The
CHALLENGER
SALE

**How to Take
Control of
the Customer
Conversation**

MATTHEW DIXON and BRENT ADAMSON

PORTFOLIO
PENGUIN

PORTFOLIO PENGUIN

Published by the Penguin Group
Penguin Books Ltd, 80 Strand, London WC2R 0RL, England
Penguin Group (USA) Inc., 375 Hudson Street, New York, New York 10014, USA
Penguin Group (Canada), 90 Eglinton Avenue East, Suite 700, Toronto, Ontario, Canada M4P 2Y3
(a division of Pearson Penguin Canada Inc.)
Penguin Ireland, 25 St Stephen's Green, Dublin 2, Ireland (a division of Penguin Books Ltd)
Penguin Group (Australia), 707 Collins Street, Melbourne, Victoria 3008, Australia
(a division of Pearson Australia Group Pty Ltd)
Penguin Books India Pvt Ltd, 11 Community Centre, Panchsheel Park, New Delhi – 110 017, India
Penguin Group (NZ), 67 Apollo Drive, Rosedale, Auckland 0632, New Zealand
(a division of Pearson New Zealand Ltd)
Penguin Books (South Africa) (Pty) Ltd, Block D, Rosebank Office Park,
181 Jan Smuts Avenue, Parktown North, Gauteng 2193, South Africa

Penguin Books Ltd, Registered Offices: 80 Strand, London WC2R 0RL, England

www.penguin.com

First published in the United States of America by Portfolio/Penguin,
a member of Penguin Group (USA) Inc. 2011
First published in Great Britain by Portfolio Penguin 2013
002

Challenger®, Challenger Rep® and Challenger Development Program® are trademarks
and service marks of The Corporate Executive Board Company

Summary description of *Situational Sales Negotiation*® training and methodology used by permission of
BayGroup International, Inc. SSN Negotiation Planner™ and © 2009 BayGroup International, Inc.
Situational Sales Negotiation® and SSN™ are trademarks and service marks of BayGroup International, Inc.

Slides from 'The Power of Planning the Unplanned' presentation used by permissions of W. W. Grainger, Inc.

Printed in Great Britain by Clays Ltd, St Ives plc

A CIP catalogue record for this book is available from the British Library

ISBN: 978–0–670–92285–7

www.greenpenguin.co.uk

Penguin Books is committed to a sustainable
future for our business, our readers and our planet.
This book is made from Forest Stewardship
Council™ certified paper.

ALWAYS LEARNING　　　　　**PEARSON**

To the members of CEB around the world,

who challenge us every day to deliver insights worthy of their

time and attention

CONTENTS

AFTERWORD

THE HISTORY OF sales has been one of steady progress interrupted by a few real breakthroughs that have changed the whole direction of the profession. These breakthroughs, marked by radical new thinking and dramatic improvements in sales results, have been rare. I can only think of three of them in the last century. The first started about a hundred years ago, when insurance companies found that they could double their sales by a simple change in selling strategy. Before this first great breakthrough, insurance policies—in common with many other products such as furniture, household goods, and capital equipment—were sold by salespeople who signed up customers and then every week visited each of them to collect premiums or installment payments. After signing up a hundred or so people, the salesperson was too busy collecting weekly premiums to do any more selling of new business. Then some anonymous genius hit on an idea that grew into what we now call the hunter-farmer model. Suppose, instead of one person both selling the policy and collecting the premiums, the two roles were split. There would be *producers,* who only sold, backed up by less experienced—and therefore cheaper—*collectors,* who came behind to look after existing customers and collect the weekly premiums. The idea was a spectacular success and it changed the insurance industry overnight. The concept quickly spread to other industries, and for the first time selling became a "pure" role, without the burden of collection.

THE SECOND BREAKTHROUGH

We don't know exactly when the producer/collector idea was first introduced, but we can be very specific about the date of the second great breakthrough. It happened in July 1925, when E. K. Strong published *The Psychology of Selling*. This seminal work introduced the idea of sales techniques, such as features and benefits, objection handling, closing, and, perhaps most important, open and closed questioning. It showed that there were things people could learn that would help them sell more effectively, and it gave rise to the sales training industry.

Looking back from the sophisticated perspective of today, many of the things Strong wrote about sound heavy-handed and simplistic. Nevertheless, he—and those who followed him—changed selling forever. Perhaps the most important aspect of his contribution was the idea that selling wasn't an innate ability. It was a set of identifiable skills that could be learned. And in 1925, that was radical indeed. It opened selling to a much wider range of people and, from anecdotal reports of the time, brought about dramatic increases in sales effectiveness.

THE THIRD BREAKTHROUGH

The third great breakthrough came in the 1970s, when researchers became interested in the idea that the techniques and skills that worked in small sales might be very different from those that worked in larger and more complex ones. I had the good fortune to be an integral part of this revolution. In the '70s I directed a huge research project, tracking 10,000 salespeople in twenty-three countries. We followed salespeople into more than 35,000 sales calls and analyzed what made some of them more successful than others in complex sales. From this twelve-year project we published a number of books, starting with *SPIN Selling*. This marked the beginning of what we now call the consultative selling era. It was a breakthrough because it introduced much more sophisticated models of how to sell complex products and services and, like the earlier breakthroughs, brought about significant gains in sales productivity.

The last thirty years have been marked by a lot of small improvements in selling, but we haven't seen many game-changing developments that could claim to be breakthroughs. True, there've been sales automation, sales process, and customer relationship management. Technology has played a bigger and bigger role in selling. There have also been huge changes to transactional selling as a result of the Internet. But all these have been incremental changes, often with questionable productivity gains, and none of them, to my way of thinking, qualifies as a bona fide breakthrough in how to sell differently and more effectively.

THE PURCHASING REVOLUTION

Interestingly, there *has* been a breakthrough development on the other side of the selling interaction. Purchasing has gone through a major revolution. From being a dead-end function in the 1980s where those who couldn't cut it in HR went to die, it has emerged as a vibrant strategic force. Armed with powerful purchasing methodologies such as supplier segmentation strategies and sophisticated supply chain management models, the rise of the new purchasing has demanded fundamental shifts in sales thinking.

I've been waiting to see how the sales world would react to the changes in purchasing. If ever there was a time for the next breakthrough, it's due in response to the purchasing revolution. But nothing big has appeared on the sales scene. It's been a bit like waiting for the inevitable earthquake. You know it's going to come someday, but you can't predict when—you just have a feeling that it's due; something is about to happen.

THE FOURTH BREAKTHROUGH?

Which brings me to *The Challenger Sale* and the work of CEB. It's too soon to know whether this is the breakthrough that we've been waiting for: Only time will tell. On the face of it, their research has all the initial signs that it may be game-changing. First, like the other examples, it flies in the face of conventional wisdom. But we need more than that. Many crazy ideas violate established thinking. What makes this different is that, like the other breakthroughs, once sales leaders understand it, they say, "Of course! It's counterintuitive, but it makes sense. I should have known." The logic you'll find in *The Challenger Sale* leads to the inescapable conclusion that this is very different thinking and it works.

I'm not going to spoil their story by telling either the details or the punch line. That's for you to read. But I will tell you why I think the research that they have done is the most important advance in selling for many years and may indeed justify the rare and coveted label of "sales breakthrough."

It's Good Research

The research is solid, and believe me, I don't say this lightly. Much of the so-called research in selling has methodological holes so big that you could fly a jumbo jet through them. We live in an age when every consultant and every author claims "research" to prove the effectiveness of what they are selling. Once research was a sure way to gain credibility; now it's fast becoming a sure way to lose it. Customers are rightly cynical about unsupportable claims that masquerade under the name of research, such as, "Our research proves that sales more than doubled after taking our training program," or "We found in our research that when salespeople used our seven customer buying styles model, it caused customer satisfaction to increase by 72 percent." Claims like these are unprovable assertions that erode the credibility of genuine research.

I was at a conference in Australia when I first heard that CEB had some startling new research on sales effectiveness. I must admit that, while I respected CEB and its good track record of solid methodology, I had been bitten enough by poor research to think to myself, "This will probably be yet another disappointment." When I got back to my office in Virginia, I invited the research team to spend a day with me and we went through their methodology with a fine-tooth comb. I admit that I confidently expected to expose serious flaws in what they had done. In particular, I had two concerns:

1. *Putting salespeople into five buckets.* The research claimed that salespeople fell into one of five distinct profiles:

> The Hard Worker
> The Challenger
> The Relationship Builder
> The Lone Wolf
> The Reactive Problem Solver

This sounded naïve and arbitrary to me. What, I asked the team, was the rationale for these five buckets? Why not seven? Or ten? They were able to show me that these were not invented categories but ones that emerged out of a massive and sophisticated statistical analysis. And they understood, in a way that many researchers don't, that their five buckets were behavioral clusters, not rigid personality types. I was satisfied that they had passed my first test.

2. *The high- versus low-performer trap.* A large percentage of the research into effective selling compares high performers with low performers. In the early years of my own research I did the same thing. As a result I learned a lot about low performers. When you ask people to compare their rock stars with their losers, you find that they can dissect the losers with surgical precision but find it hard, if not impossible, to put their finger on exactly what makes their rock stars rock. I soon learned that I ended up with a detailed understanding of poor performance and not much else. If my research was to have any meaning I had to compare top performers with average, or core, performers. It was reassuring to find that CEB research had adopted exactly that approach.

It's Based on an Impressive Sample

It's common for sales research to be based on small samples of fifty to eighty participants drawn from just three or four companies. Larger-scale research is harder to do and significantly more expensive. My own research had used samples of a thousand or more, not because we liked megastudies but because—given the noisy data of real-life selling—we had no choice if we wanted to draw statistically meaningful insights. The initial sample in the Challenger research was 700, which has since grown to 6,000. That's impressive by any standard. What's even more impressive is that ninety companies participated in the research. With a sample this wide we can rule out many of the factors that normally prevent research from generalizing its results to cover selling as a whole. CEB findings are not about a particular organization or a specific industry. They apply across the whole spectrum of selling, and that's important.

It Didn't Find What the Researchers Expected

I always mistrust research that finds exactly what it seeks. Researchers, like everybody else, have a bundle of prejudices and preconceived ideas. If they know what they are looking for, by gosh they will find it. I was really pleased to hear that the researchers themselves were stunned to discover that their results were almost the opposite of what they had expected. That's a very healthy sign and a frequent characteristic of significant research. Look again at their five profiles:

> The Hard Worker
> The Challenger
> The Relationship Builder
> The Lone Wolf
> The Reactive Problem Solver

Most sales executives, if they were forced to choose just one profile to make up their sales force, would have chosen the Relationship Builder, and that's just what the research team was expecting to find. Think again. The research showed that Relationship Builders were unlikely to be star performers. In contrast, the Challengers, who are awkward to manage and assertive both with customers and with their own managers, came out on top. As you'll see in the book, Challengers won out not by a small margin but a massive one. And the margin was far greater in complex sales.

THE DECLINE OF RELATIONSHIP SELLING

How can we explain these counterintuitive findings? In the book, Matt Dixon and Brent Adamson build a very persuasive case. Let me add my own two cents' worth to what they say. Conventional wisdom has long held that selling is about relationships and that in complex sales, relationships are the underpinning of all sales success. Yet over the last ten years there have been some disturbing hints that relationship-based selling may be less effective than it used to be. My own studies of what customers value from salespeople would be a good example. When we asked 1,100 customers what they valued in salespeople, we were surprised at how few times they mentioned relationships. It seems that the old advice, "Build relationships first and then sales will follow," no longer holds true. That's not to say that relationships are unimportant. I think a better explanation is that the relationship and the purchasing decision have become decoupled. Today you'll often hear customers say, "I have a great relationship with this sales rep but I buy from her competition because they provide better value." Personally, I believe that a customer relationship is the *result* and not the cause of successful selling. It is a reward that the salesperson earns by creating customer value. If you help customers think differently and bring them new ideas—which is what the Challenger rep does—then you earn the right to a relationship.

THE CHALLENGE OF CHALLENGE

At the heart of this book is the demonstrated superiority of Challengers in terms of customer impact and therefore sales results. Many people are taken aback by this finding—and I suspect some readers will feel the same. But while the articulation of the Challenger idea is new, the evidence has been visible all around us. Surveys of customers consistently show that they put the highest value on salespeople who make them think, who bring new ideas, who find creative and innovative ways to help the customer's business. In recent years, customers have been demanding more depth and expertise. They expect salespeople to teach them things they don't know. These are the core skills of Challengers. They are the skills of the future, and any sales force that ignores the message of this book does so at its peril.

I've been in the business of sales innovation all my professional life, so I don't anticipate that the publication of this important research will bring an instant revolution. Change is slow and painful. But I do know this: There will be a few companies that will take the findings that are laid out here and will implement them well. Those companies will reap huge gains and significant competitive advantage from building Challenge into their sales force. As CEB research shows, we live in an era when product innovation alone cannot be the basis for corporate success. How you sell has become more important than what you sell. An effective sales force is a more sustainable competitive advantage than a great product stream. This book gives you a well-articulated blueprint for building a winning sales force. My advice is this: Read it, think about it, implement it. You, and your organization, will be glad that you did.

Professor Neil Rackham
Author of *SPIN Selling*

The
CHALLENGER
SALE

A SURPRISING LOOK INTO THE FUTURE

IN THE UNFORGETTABLE early months of 2009, as the bottom fell out of the global economy, business-to-business sales leaders around the world faced an epic problem and an even deeper mystery.

Customers had vanished overnight. Commerce had ground to a halt. Credit was scarce, and cash even scarcer. For anyone in business, times were tough. But for heads of sales, they were an absolute nightmare. Imagine having to get up every morning, rally your troops, and send them into a battle they couldn't possibly win. To find business where none could be found. True, sales has always been about the good fight— about winning business often in the face of strong resistance. But this was different. It's one thing to sell to reluctant, even nervous customers. It's another thing altogether to sell to no one at all. And that's where we were in early 2009.

Yet therein lay the mystery. Staring directly into the teeth of the toughest sales environment in decades—if not ever—a small but uniquely gifted number of sales reps *were* selling. In fact, they were selling a lot. While others struggled to close even the smallest of deals, these individuals were bringing in the kind of business most reps could only dream of even in an up economy. Were they lucky? Were they just born with it? And most important, how could you possibly capture that magic, bottle it, and export it to everyone else? For many companies, their very survival depended on the answer.

It was into this environment that CEB launched what has become one of the most important studies of sales rep productivity in decades. Tasked by members of CEB's sales program—heads of sales from the world's largest, best-known companies—we set out to identify what exactly set this very special group of sales reps apart. And having now studied that question intensively for the better part of four years, spanning dozens of companies and thousands of sales reps, we have discovered three core insights that have fundamentally rewritten the sales playbook and led B2B sales executives all over the world to think very differently about how they sell.

The first insight was something we weren't originally even looking for. It turns out that just about every B2B sales rep in the world falls into one of five distinct profiles, a specific set of skills and behaviors that define his or her primary mode of interacting with customers. Now, that's interesting in and of itself, as you'll be able to find yourself and your colleagues in these profiles when you see them. These five profiles prove to be an incredibly practical way of dividing the world into a manageable set of alternative sales techniques.

That said, it's really the second insight that changes everything. When you take those five profiles and compare them with actual sales performance, you find there is a very clear winner and a very clear loser: One of them spectacularly outperforms the other four, while one of them falls dramatically behind. Yet there is something very disturbing about these results. When we show them to sales leaders, we hear the same thing again and again. These leaders find the results deeply troubling, because they've placed by far their biggest bet on the profile least likely to win. This one insight has shattered the way many sales leaders think about the kind of reps they need to survive and thrive in a tough economy.

And that brings us to the third and final core insight from this work— arguably the most explosive of them all. As we dug deeper into the data, we found something even more surprising. While we'd set out four years ago to find the winning recipe for sales rep success in a down economy, all of the data indicate something far more important. The profile most likely to win isn't winning *because* of the down economy, but *irrespective* of it. These reps are winning because they've mastered the complex sale, not because they've mastered a complex economy. In other words, when we unlocked the mystery of high performance in the down economy, the story turned out to be much bigger than anyone had anticipated. Your very best sales reps—the ones who carried you through the downturn— aren't just the heroes of today, but are also the heroes of tomorrow, as they are far better able to drive sales and deliver customer value in *any* kind of economic environment. What we ultimately found is a dramatically improved recipe for a successful solution sales rep.

We call these winning reps Challengers, and this is their story.

THE EVOLVING JOURNEY OF SOLUTION SELLING

IN EARLY 2009, CEB set out to answer the most pressing question on the minds of sales leaders at the time: How can we sell our way through the worst economy in decades?

It was a question naturally accompanied not only by urgent concern—even fear—but also by a sense of real mystery. In a world where B2B selling had ground to nearly a complete halt, sales executives were surprised to find a handful of reps still bringing in business typical of the best of times, not the worst. But what were they doing differently? How were these reps still selling well when virtually no one else was selling at all?

In studying this question in significant depth we discovered something surprising. What set these best reps apart wasn't so much their ability to succeed in a down economy, but their ability to succeed in a complex sales model—one that places a huge burden on both reps and customers to think and behave differently. That model is often referred to as "solution selling" or a "solutions approach"—or simply "solutions"—and has come to dominate sales and marketing strategy across the last ten to twenty years.

The story we found in our research, however, told us something very important about the world of solution selling. It's evolving dramatically. As suppliers seek to sell ever bigger, more complex, disruptive, and expensive "solutions," B2B customers are naturally buying with greater care and reluctance than ever before, dramatically rewriting the purchasing playbook in the process. As a result, traditional, time-tested sales techniques no longer work the way they used to. Core-performing reps struggle mightily in all but the most straightforward of sales, leaving an alarming number of half-completed deals in their wake as they attempt to adapt to changing customer demands and evolving buying behaviors.

From this perspective, the down economy that so troubled senior sales executives when we first launched this work proved to be a red herring. The downturn exacerbated the widening gap between core- and star-performing reps, but it didn't cause it. In fact, the story laid out here isn't about the economy at all. It's about the evolving world of solution selling and the skills necessary to drive commercial success across the foreseeable future irrespective of economic conditions. As the world of solution selling continues to change, our research clearly indicates that a specific set of sales rep skills has emerged as significantly more likely to drive commercial results than those emphasized in either traditional product selling or early solution selling. To understand why those skills matter so much, it's helpful to first examine the evolution of the sales model itself.

THE PATH TO SOLUTION SELLING

Solution selling comes in many flavors, but generally describes the migration from a focus on transactional sales of individual products (usually based on price or volume) to a focus on broad-based consultative sales of "bundles" of products and services. The key to its success is the creation of bundled offerings that not only meet broader customer needs in a unique and valuable way, but also that competitors can't easily replicate. The best solutions, therefore, are not just unique, but sustainably so, allowing a supplier to address customer challenges in either new or more economical ways relative to the competition.

Why does that matter? Solution selling is largely driven by suppliers' attempts to escape dramatically increasing commoditization pressure as individual products and services become less differentiated over time. Because it is harder for a competitor to offer the full spectrum of capabilities comprising a well-designed solution bundle, it's much easier to protect premium pricing in a solution sale than in a traditional product sale.

Not surprisingly, the approach has become widely popular across business-to-business sales for that reason. In fact, to get a sense of how widespread solution selling has become, in a recent survey we asked sales leaders to characterize their primary sales strategy across a multi-step continuum from traditional product sales on one end to full-on customized solution selling on the other. The result? Fully three-quarters of respondents reported aspirations to be some kind of solutions provider to a majority of their customers. Essentially, some flavor of solution selling has become a dominant sales strategy across almost every industry.

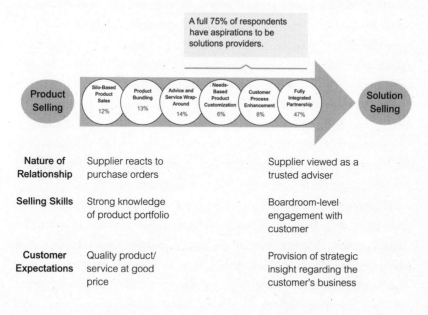

Figure 1.1. The Shift from Product to Solution Selling

Now, we don't dispute the value of this long-term migration to solution selling—particularly as a way to escape relentless commoditization pressure—but the strategy nonetheless brings with it a number of real challenges. Chief among them are two challenges that explain how—and why—the solutions model has necessarily evolved over time. The first is the burden that solutions places on the customer. The second is the burden it places on the rep.

THE CUSTOMER BURDEN OF SOLUTIONS

By definition, a shift to solution selling results in customers' expecting you to actually "solve" a real problem and not just supply a reliable product. And that's hard to do. It requires that you not only understand the customer's underlying problems or challenges as well if not better than they do themselves, but also that you can identify new and better means of addressing those challenges, articulate clear benefits from using limited resources to solve that problem versus competing ones, and determine the right metrics to measure success. And the only way to do all of that is to ask the customer lots of questions. So reps spend a great deal of time asking things like, "What's keeping you up at night?" in an attempt to truly understand a customer's competing challenges.

The problem with all of this "discovery" is that it can often take on the feel of a protracted ping-pong match between the supplier and customer. The customer explains their needs, the rep summarizes her understanding, the customer confirms whether or not the rep got it right, she creates a proposal, the customer reviews and amends it, and on and on.

This complicated and often rather protracted process requires a huge amount of customer involvement at each stage, placing two kinds of burden on the customer: The first is time, and the second is timing. Not only does this dance entail significant customer commitment across a wide range of different stakeholders, conference calls, and presentations, but from the customer's point of view, most of this effort comes early, before they see any value. Really, it's an act of faith on their part that they're going to get anything in return for all of their trouble.

This has led to something we call "solutions fatigue." As solutions complexity has increased, this burden on customers has gone up as well, leading customers to engage with suppliers very differently when it comes to complex deals. In fact, four trends really stand out in describing how customer buying behavior is evolving rapidly.

The Rise of the Consensus-Based Sale

First, we have seen a significant increase in the need for consensus in order to get deals done. Because the payoff of buying a complex solution is so uncertain, even C-level executives with significant decision-making authority are unwilling to go out on a limb to make a large purchase decision without the support of their teams. Our research indicates that widespread support for a supplier across their team is the number-one thing senior decision makers look for in making a purchase decision (a finding we'll discuss in more depth later in this book).

And of course, that need for consensus has huge implications for sales productivity. Not only does the rep now have to spend the time tracking down all these individuals and selling them on the solution, but the risk that at least one of them is going to say no goes up with each new stakeholder that rep has to engage.

Increased Risk Aversion

Second, as deals have become more complex and more expensive, most customers have become much more concerned about whether they'll *ever* see a return on their investment. As a result, many are moving aggressively to require suppliers to share more deeply in the perceived higher risk of these solutions themselves. It's nothing new for customers to demand just-in-time delivery or on-demand production, but more and more we're seeing revisions to the very metrics customers use to judge the success of a solution implementation. As a result, in the world of complex solutions, supplier success is often measured by the performance of the customer's business, not the supplier's products.

Suppliers looking to grow a solutions business, then, are going to have to run right at risk, building it directly into their value proposition, as an increasingly large number of customers are no longer willing to accept at face value that "solutions" will ultimately deliver the kind of value that suppliers promise up front.

Greater Demand for Customization

Third, as deal complexity goes up, so does customers' natural tendency to want to modify the deal to more closely meet their specific needs. Whereas suppliers typically see customization purely from a cost perspective, customers see customization as part of the promise of a "solutions" sale: "If you're going to 'solve' my problem, then this is what I need it to do. Why should that cost more money? After all, if it doesn't do that, then it's not really a 'solution,' is it?" It's hard to argue with that kind of logic. Customization: Everyone wants it; no one wants to pay for it.

The Rise of Third-Party Consultants

Finally, over the last several years, we've seen a dramatic and troubling rise in the number of third-party consultants employed by customers to help them "extract maximum value from the purchase decision." A well-established practice in some sectors—corporate health insurance in the United States, for example—this trend really took off globally in late 2009, forged by the need of most companies to cut costs on the one hand, and the even more urgent need of recently laid-off industry experts to find a job on the other. Typically, these newly minted consultants sold their services largely on the basis of their ability to save companies money. In that case, "extracting maximum value from the purchase decision" really was nothing more than code for doing everything possible to stick it to suppliers on price, up to and including going back and auditing prior deals to uncover grounds for renegotiation.

Over time, however, larger organizational players have become deeply involved in the purchase as well. In their case, "extracting maximum value from the purchase decision" typically translates into something closer to helping customers navigate solutions complexity. The fact of the matter is that as suppliers seek to sell increasingly broad solutions to ever more complex customer problems, as often as not the complexity of those problems is so high that customers are themselves unqualified to navigate—let alone evaluate—potential courses of action on their own. They need help. Rather than turning to the suppliers for that help, however, they look to "neutral" third-party experts.

As a result, suppliers today are frequently confronted with new and aggressive third-party intermediaries looking to take their share of "value" from the deal. And you can be sure that that pound of flesh is going to come from the supplier side, not the customer side, given whom these consultants are working for. In this world, you can easily wind up with all the customer's business, but none of their money.

All four of these trends in customer buying behavior have led to a hard truth for sales organizations all over the world—and especially for the reps who sell for them: While the economy has gotten better, selling hasn't gotten any easier. It's the physics of sales: Suppliers called the solutions play, and customers have made their countermove. Customers are looking for ways to reduce both the complexity and the risk that suppliers' solution selling efforts have foisted upon them.

A WIDENING TALENT GAP

How does this solutions story play out for individual rep performance? The impact has been nothing short of dramatic.

In a recent study, we conducted an analysis looking at the impact of a company's sales model—in other words, transactional selling versus solution selling—on the performance distribution of their sales reps. What we found was eye-opening and more than a little troubling.

In a transactional selling environment, the performance gap between average and star performers is 59 percent. So the star performer sells about one and a half times as much as the core performer. However, in companies with solution selling models the distribution is very different. There, they outperform by almost *200 percent*. The gap is four times greater. Put another way, as sales become more complex, the gap between core and star performers widens dramatically.

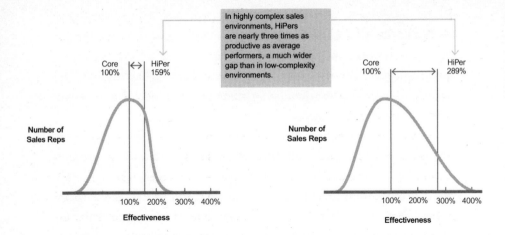

Source: CEB, CEB Sales Leadership Council, 2011.

Figure 1.2. Core Versus High Performers in Transactional (Left) and Solution Selling (Right) Environments

This leads us to three conclusions. First, as a solutions provider, you've got to find a way to put a big corporate bear hug around your stars. They're carrying the day for you. One head of sales in business services told us recently that of their hundred sales reps, *two* were responsible for bringing in 80 percent of the company's revenue. While the situation in your organization may not be as extreme, the shift to solution selling has undoubtedly seen a dramatic rise in key-person dependency problems across many sales forces. It's not just that stars are carrying the day for you; they're often carrying the entire company.

Second, as your sales model becomes more complex, the value of narrowing the gap between your core and star performers goes up radically. In the transactional world, the value of getting someone just halfway from good to great is a 30 percent improvement. That's not bad. But the value of the same move in a solutions environment is an almost 100 percent improvement. Put simply, closing that gap is worth a lot more than it used to be.

Finally, the penalty for not closing the gap is terrifying. As your model evolves, left untended, the core will fall farther and farther behind, until they ultimately can't execute the new model at all.

A NEW WAY FORWARD

In this world of dramatically changing customer buying behavior and rapidly diverging sales talent, your sales approach must evolve or you will be left behind.

So the question now is: What do you do about it? If you're going to win going forward, you've got to equip reps to generate new demand in a world of reluctant, risk-averse customers—customers who are struggling to buy complex solutions just as much as you are struggling to sell them. That's going to take a very special kind of sales professional indeed. As the world of sales has evolved dramatically across the last ten to twenty years, our research indicates that the best reps have evolved a set of unique and powerful skills to keep up. And that's where our story goes next.

THE CHALLENGER (PART 1):
A NEW MODEL FOR HIGH PERFORMANCE

THE NEED TO understand what your star-performing reps are doing to set themselves apart from their core-performing colleagues has never been more urgent. The world of sales is changing. The pre-recession recipe for sales success won't get the job done in a post-recession economy. That said, the economy itself serves only as a backdrop to this story. The real story revolves around the dramatic change in customer buying behaviors across the last five years that we reviewed in the previous chapter—all in response to suppliers' efforts to sell larger, more complex, more disruptive, and more expensive solutions.

Still, if nothing else, the global economic collapse served to throw the widening gap between core and star reps into stark contrast. Even in the depths of the downturn, when most reps were far behind quota, some reps—quite inexplicably—still managed not just to hit their goals, but to exceed them. What were they doing differently? Generally, the tendency in sales is to simply chalk up the difference to natural talent and assume stars are just born with it. It's not as if you can just take their skill, bottle it, and sprinkle it over your core performers to close the gap. Right?

Well, what if you could? What if you could track down the replicable part of what truly sets star performers apart, capture that magic, and export it to the rest of your sales organization? Imagine a world where all your reps—or at least many more of them—performed like stars. What would that be worth to you? What would it mean for the overall performance of your company?

Well, in 2009, in a world where only the stars were selling to begin with, it could mean the difference between bankruptcy and survival. And it was in this high-stakes world that we first set out to answer the question: Which skills, behaviors, knowledge, and attitudes matter most for high performance?

IN SEARCH OF ANSWERS

To figure this out, we surveyed hundreds of frontline sales managers across ninety companies around the world, asking those managers to assess three reps each from their teams—two average performers and one star performer—along forty-four different attributes. And while the initial model was built on an analysis of the first 700 reps for whom we had data—representing every major industry, geography, and go-to-market model—we've since increased that number to well over 6,000 reps all over the world as we continue to run this diagnostic survey. Among other things, continuing that work has allowed us to determine whether or not the story in the data has changed over time, especially in light of the recent slow but steady economic recovery. And for reasons we'll review momentarily, we've been able to establish quite clearly that these findings hold true irrespective of economic conditions.

So what exactly was in this survey? The table on page 16 provides a sample of the rep attributes we tested as part of this work. We asked managers to assess attitudes, including the degree to which their reps seek to resolve customer issues and their willingness to risk disapproval. We asked about skills and behaviors, like the reps' level of business acumen and needs-diagnosis ability. We looked at activities, like reps' tendency to follow the sales process and thoroughly evaluate opportunities. And, finally, we asked about reps' knowledge of their customers' industry as well as their own companies' products.

PARTIAL SAMPLE OF VARIABLES TESTED			
ATTITUDES	**SKILLS/BEHAVIORS**	**ACTIVITIES**	**KNOWLEDGE**
Desire to seek issue resolution	Business acumen	Sales process adherence	Industry knowledge
Willingness to risk disapproval	Customer-needs assessment	Evaluation of opportunities	Product knowledge
Accessibility	Communication	Preparation	
Goal motivation	Use of internal resources	Lead generation	
Extent of outcome focus	Negotiation	Administration	
Attachment to the company	Relationship management		
Curiosity	Solution selling		
Discretionary effort	Teamwork		

In terms of demographics, the study covered a wide range of selling models, everything from hunters to farmers, field reps to inside sales reps, key account managers to broad-based account reps, as well as both direct sellers and indirect sellers. That said, we carefully controlled for things like rep tenure, geography, and account size to make sure that the results apply not only universally across the entire sample, but also broadly across the wide range of the companies represented in our membership.

Finally, because we were working with sales reps, we had a very practical means of measuring actual performance, namely each individual rep's performance against goal. When you put it all together, what all of this work gives you is a very robust data-driven snapshot of rep performance that allows you to answer the question, "Of all the things a sales rep *could* do well, which ones actually matter most for sales performance?" It's an extremely thorough picture of what "good" looks like when it comes to sales rep skill and behavior.

We should also point out what we did *not* study. This work is definitively not an examination of sales rep personality types or personal strengths. That kind of thing is hard to measure and even harder to do anything about. If we were to tell you that "charisma" is hugely important to sales success, you might not disagree, but you'd likely struggle to know what to actually *do* with that information. Sure, over time you might find new homes for all of your noncharismatic reps and hire more outgoing ones instead. But while that may in fact help performance tomorrow, it would be awfully difficult to execute practically, in order to improve performance today. Instead, first and foremost, we wanted to provide advice around what you can do right now with the reps you *already* have (though there is certainly a hiring story that comes out of these results as well).

To that end, looking back at the list of variables, you'll notice that all of the attributes we tested were focused on reps' *demonstrated behaviors*. In other words, how much more or less likely is a rep to do "X"? Or how effective is a rep at doing "Y"? We did that because skills and behaviors *are* things you can do something about right away. You may or may not be charismatic, but through better coaching, for example, I can help you do a better job of following the sales process. Or, through better training and tools, I can improve your product or industry knowledge.

This is a survey about getting things done. It wasn't designed so much to determine why your stars are better, but rather to determine how to make your core better. Think of the potentially huge commercial value currently locked up in the middle 60 percent of your sales force. What would it be worth to make each of those reps even just a little bit better? Our survey focused on the things you can do right now to help the core performers you already have act more like the stars that you wish they were.

So what did we find? Which of these many attributes matters most? At the highest level, the story revolves around three key findings, each representing a radical departure from how most sales executives think about how to drive sales success. Let's take them one by one.

FINDING #1:
THERE ARE FIVE TYPES OF SALES REPS

The first thing we did was to run a factor analysis on the data. Put simply, factor analysis is a statistical methodology for grouping a large number of variables into a smaller set of categories within which variables co-present and move together. For example, if we were studying ecosystems, a factor analysis of every potential ecosystem variable would tell us that things like intense heat, sand, arid conditions, scorpions, and cacti tend to co-present in nature. Because we tend to find them together, we could give this category a name, i.e., "a desert."

When we ran factor analysis on the data from our sales rep study, we found something really intriguing. The analysis indicated very clearly that certain rep characteristics tend to clump together. The forty-four attributes we tested fell into five distinct groups, each containing a very different combination of rep characteristics. When a rep tends to be good at one attribute in that group, he or she is very likely to be good at all of the others in that group as well.

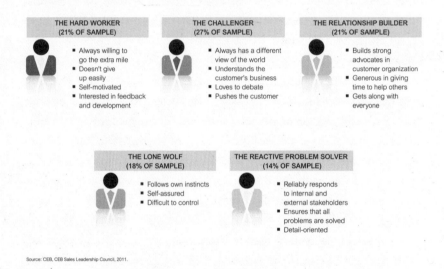

Source: CEB, CEB Sales Leadership Council, 2011.

Figure 2.1. The Five Sales Rep Profiles

Figure 2.1 shows these five distinct rep profiles as well as the descriptive variables that are clustered within each. These groups are not necessarily mutually exclusive. Going back to the ecosystem example earlier, think of it this way: All deserts have intense heat and sand, but intense heat and sand are not unique to deserts. You find these things in other ecosystems too, maybe just in different abundance. In our study, every rep has at least a baseline level of performance across all the attributes we tested. For example, to one degree or another, all sales reps adhere to a formal sales process. All reps have at least a minimum acceptable level of product and industry knowledge. But for almost every rep, a specific subset of these attributes defines their primary approach to customers.

We like to think of these profiles as college or university degrees. In order to graduate, every student must cover a broad core curriculum: science, language, history, math, etc. But at the same time, university students have a "primary" or "major" as well—the thing they specialize in that sets them apart. And that's what these five profiles are all about. They are the five distinct "majors" in sales.

These five profiles are not groups that we put together based on our interpretation of the data or our view of the world. We let the analysis tell the story. The five profiles are statistically derived, but they accurately and completely describe the five most common profiles found in the real world. Interestingly, they're relatively evenly distributed across our sample population.

So who are these different reps? As we go through the five profiles, ask yourself the following questions: Which of these five profiles do you think best describes the bulk of your sales force? Where have you placed your bets as an organization or, perhaps more practically speaking, which type of rep are you trying to recruit right now? Which are you trying to get your reps to behave more like?

The Hard Worker

Hard Workers are exactly who they sound like. These are the reps who show up early, stay late, and are always willing to put in the extra effort. They're the "nose to the grindstone" sellers. They're self-motivated and don't give up easily. They'll make more calls in an hour and conduct more visits in a week than just about anyone else on the team. And they enthusiastically and frequently seek out feedback, always looking for opportunities to improve their game.

A CSO at a global logistics company put it like this: "These guys believe that doing the right things the right way will inevitably get you results. If they do enough calls, send enough e-mails, and respond to enough RFPs [requests for proposal], it'll all come together by the end of the quarter. They're the ones who were actually paying attention when we pounded the importance of sales process."

The Relationship Builder

Just as the name implies, Relationship Builders are all about building and nurturing strong personal and professional relationships and advocates across the customer organization. They're very generous with their time and work very hard to ensure that customers' needs are met. Their primary posture with customers is largely one of accessibility and service. "Whatever you need," they'll tell customers, "I'm here to make that happen. Just say the word."

Not surprisingly, one VP of sales we recently interviewed told us, "Our customers *love* our relationship builders. They've worked very hard to build customer relationships, sometimes over years. It feels like that's really made a huge difference to our business."

The Lone Wolf

The Lone Wolf will look familiar to anyone in sales. Lone Wolves are deeply self-confident. As a result, they tend to follow their own instincts instead of the rules. In many ways, the Lone Wolves are the "prima donnas" of the sales force—the "cowboys" who do things "their way" or not at all. More often than not they drive sales leaders crazy—they have no process compliance, no trip reports, no CRM (customer relationship management) entries.

"Frankly," one head of sales told us, "I'd fire them if I could, but I can't, because they're all crushing their numbers." And that's the case for most companies. On average, Lone Wolves tend to do very well despite egregiously flouting the system, because if they didn't do well, they'd probably have been fired already.

The Reactive Problem Solver

The Reactive Problem Solver is highly reliable and very detail-oriented. While every rep in one way or another is focused on solving customer problems, these individuals are naturally drawn to ensuring that all of the promises that are inevitably made as part of a sale are actually kept once that deal is done. They tend to focus very heavily on post-sales follow-up, ensuring that service issues around implementation and execution are addressed quickly and thoroughly.

One CEB member described the problem solver as "a customer service rep in sales rep clothing." As she put it, "They come into the office in the morning with grand plans to generate new sales, but as soon as an existing customer calls with a problem, they dive right in rather than passing it to the people we actually pay to solve those problems. They find ways to make that customer happy, but at the expense of finding ways to generate more business."

The Challenger

Challengers are the debaters on the team. They've got a deep understanding of the customer's business and use that understanding to push the customer's thinking and teach them something new about how their company can compete more effectively. They're not afraid to share their views, even when they're different and potentially controversial. Challengers are assertive—they tend to "press" customers a little—both on their thinking and around things like pricing. And as many sales leaders will tell you, they don't reserve their Challenger mentality for customers alone. They tend to push their own managers and senior leaders within their own organizations as well. Not in an annoying or aggressive manner, mind you—then we'd simply have to call this profile "the Jerk"—but in a way that forces people to think about complex issues from a different perspective.

As one member put it, "We have a handful of Challengers in our company, and almost all of them seem to have a standing time slot on our CSO's calendar to discuss what they're seeing and hearing in the market. The CSO loves it. They're constantly bringing fresh insight to the table that forces him to constantly check his strategy against reality."

FINDING #2:
ONE CLEAR WINNER AND ONE CLEAR LOSER

If you step back and look at the five profiles, ask yourself: Which would you prefer to have on your team? In many ways, they all look good.

But as interesting as it is that reps fall into one of five distinct profiles, it's really the second finding that's proven so completely surprising. When you take these five profiles and compare them to actual sales performance, you find something very dramatic. One in particular performs head and shoulders above the other four, and one falls dramatically behind, yet the results go against conventional wisdom. When most sales leaders see how each profile performs, they tell you quite frankly, they've indeed placed their biggest bet on the profile least likely to win.

So who wins? The answer is the Challenger by a landslide. Take a look at figure 2.2.

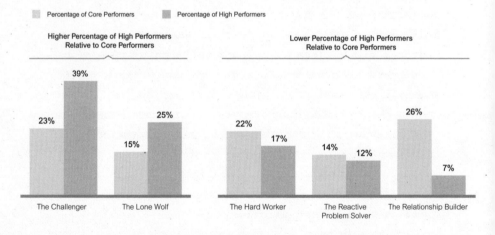

Figure 2.2. Core and High Performers by Profile

In comparing the five rep profiles with actual sales performance, the first thing we did was separate core performers from star performers and analyze each independently. To determine star performers, we asked participating companies to tell us which of their reps in the sample fell into the top 20 percent of their sales force as measured by performance against goal. Once we had categorized all the reps in our sample by performance, we then determined the distribution of each group across the five profiles. And what we found was fascinating.

First, the distribution of *core* performers across the five profiles is fairly even. No profile dominates among average sales reps. It turns out core performers aren't average because they gravitate to a specific profile; they're average because well, they're average. They show up in all five categories and achieve average performance in every single one. In other words, there's not one way to be average, but five. Mediocrity comes in multiple flavors. Indeed, you see this in figure 2.2 in the relatively even distribution of the lighter-shaded bars across the five profiles.

But when you look at the distribution of *star* performers across these same five profiles, you find something completely different. While there may be five ways to be average, there's clearly a dominant way to be a star. And that, by far, is the Challenger profile, comprising nearly 40 percent of all high performers in our study.

You'll remember that the Challenger rep is the rep who loves to debate. The one who uses his or her deep understanding of a customer's business not simply to serve them, but to teach them: to push their thinking and provide them with new and different ways to think about their business and how to compete.

So what truly sets them apart? In our analysis, of the forty-four or so attributes we tested, six of them showed up as statistically significant in defining someone as a Challenger rep:

- Offers the customer unique perspectives
- Has strong two-way communication skills
- Knows the individual customer's value drivers
- Can identify economic drivers of the customer's business
- Is comfortable discussing money
- Can pressure the customer

At first glance, this list may seem like a strange mix of unrelated qualities. In fact, when we first put together the list of attributes to be tested, it's unlikely anyone would have picked these particular six as the key components of star performance. Nonetheless, that's how the analysis came out. Each of these attributes represents a particular way in which Challenger reps significantly outperform their colleagues in the core.

That said, if we group the attributes into three categories we find they paint a very clear picture of who the Challenger truly is. A Challenger is really defined by the ability to do three things: teach, tailor, and take control:

- With their unique perspective on the customer's business and their ability to engage in robust two-way dialogue, Challengers are able to *teach for differentiation* during the sales interaction.
- Because Challengers possess a superior sense of a customer's economic and value drivers, they are able to *tailor for resonance,* delivering the right message to the right person within the customer organization.
- Finally, Challengers are comfortable discussing money and can, when needed, press the customer a bit. In this way, the Challenger *takes control* of the sale.

These are the defining attributes of the Challenger—the ability to teach, to tailor, and to take control. They're the pillars of what we've come to call the Challenger Selling Model, and the rest of this book will provide a road map for building these capabilities in your sales force.

Before we turn to a closer analysis of Challengers, however, let's return briefly to our overall results. Because as big an ah-ha! as it has been for sales leaders around the world that the Challenger is so much more likely to win than any other profile, it's proven equally surprising—and frankly much more troubling—for sales executives to learn that the Relationship Builder falls so far behind. In our study, only *7 percent* of all star performers fell into the Relationship Builder profile, far fewer than any other. And this finding should be a real red flag for all sales leaders encouraging their reps to simply go out and "build deeper relationships" with customers, or, as one company told their reps in the depths of the recession, to go out and "hug your customers."

Now, before we go any further, we should emphasize that these results by no means suggest that customer relationships aren't important for sales—this would be a naïve conclusion. Of course they are important, particularly in complex sales where reps are required to engage in relationships with multiple stakeholders. If your customers don't know who you are, or worse, outright dislike you, you must fix that first. But at the same time, if your strategy as a sales rep is largely one of being available to take care of whatever your customer needs—of acquiescing to the customer's every demand—that can be a recipe for disaster in an environment where your customers are more reluctant than ever to buy your solutions for all the reasons we discussed in chapter 1. In that environment, as critical as a strong customer relationship may be, familiarity alone isn't enough to win the business. A service-oriented quarterly check-in call with your customer can be a great way to *find* business, but it's not a very good way to *make* business. As a result, in a world where findable business has all but vanished, Relationship Builders are doomed to fail.

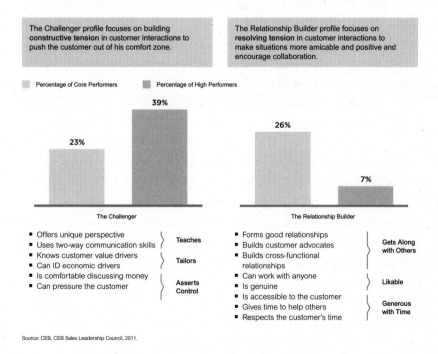

Figure 2.3. Challenger Versus Relationship Builder Profile

So is the Challenger profile really all that different from that of the Relationship Builder? It absolutely is. When you look at the attributes that define the Challenger and compare them with the ones that define the Relationship Builder, as we've depicted in figure 2.3, you'll see why.

Challenger reps succeed for all of the reasons we just discussed—they excel at teaching, tailoring, and taking control. Meanwhile, as the Challenger is focused on pushing the customer out of their comfort zone, the Relationship Builder is focused on being accepted into it. They focus on building strong personal relationships across the customer organization, being likable and generous with their time. The Relationship Builder adopts a service mentality. While the Challenger is focused on customer value, the Relationship Builder is more concerned with customer convenience.

The Challenger rep wins by maintaining a certain amount of constructive tension across the sale. The Relationship Builder, on the other hand, strives to resolve or defuse tension, not create it. It's the exact opposite approach. Granted, the conversation with the Relationship Builder is in most cases a very professional one, but it doesn't really *help* the customer make progress against their goals. They're likable, but they're not very effective. The Challenger, by contrast, knows that there is value for both you and your customers in maintaining that tension a little bit longer in a manner that pushes the customer to think differently about their own business—about the ways in which you might be able to help them (to save money or make money) and, ultimately, about the value you provide as a supplier.

Here's how a global head of sales in the hospitality industry put it when he saw these results: "You know, this is really hard to look at. For the last ten years, it's been our stated strategy to hire effective Relationship Builders. After all, we're in the hospitality business. And for a while, that worked fine. But ever since the economy crashed, my Relationship Builders are completely lost. They can't sell a thing. And as I look at this, I now know why."

FINDING #3:
CHALLENGERS ARE THE SOLUTION SELLING REP, NOT JUST THE DOWN ECONOMY REP

The dramatic difference between Challengers and all other reps brings us to our third and arguably most dramatic finding. Almost inevitably at this point in our story, a question naturally comes up about the "staying power" of the Challenger profile. After all, we first derived these findings at a very specific and uniquely bad moment of economic performance. So is it possible that the superior performance of Challengers is simply a temporary phenomenon—a product of the Great Recession and the brutal sales environment it engendered? If that's the case, are we likely to come back in two or three years and find that some other profile—perhaps one as yet unidentified—is more likely to win? Based on what we're seeing in the data, we don't believe that's the case. To show you why, let's shift our perspective to the longer view for a moment and look at the Challenger findings in the context of the broader shift toward solution selling.

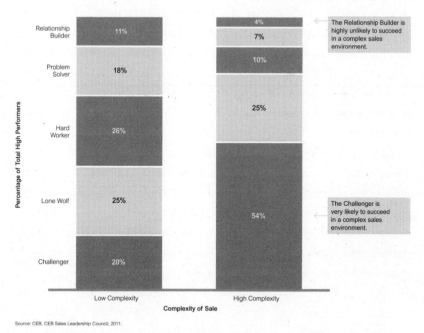

Source: CEB, CEB Sales Leadership Council, 2011.

Figure 2.4. High Performance by Sales Rep Profile in Low- and High-Complexity Sales Environments

If we look at the data through a different lens—the lens of sales complexity—we find something even more dramatic. After our initial analysis, we went back to the data and divided up the high performers according to the complexity of the deals they were selling (see figure 2.4), comparing star performers who sell relatively simple, stand-alone products across a shorter sales cycle versus those who sell more complex bundles of products and solutions across a relatively longer sales cycle.

In complex sales, Challengers absolutely dominate, with *more than 50 percent* of all star performers falling into this category. The only group that can even come close are the Lone Wolves—who, most sales leaders will agree, are hard to find and even harder to control. At the same time, Relationship Builders nearly fall off the map entirely—the likelihood that they achieve star status when you're selling complex solutions falls to *nearly zero*.

This explains why so many organizations struggle with the migration to solutions. The world of solution selling is almost definitionally about a disruptive sale. It's not that you're asking customers to buy your product and put it up on the shelf with all of the other products they've bought. Rather, you're asking customers to change their behavior—to stop acting in one way and starting acting in another. To make that happen, however, you have to get customers to think differently about how they operate. You need to show them a new way to think about their business. From that perspective, it's really no surprise that in this more complex world only one profile wins—and it wins by a country mile.

If you're not building or hiring Challenger reps, chances are you're going to come up well short as your deals become more complex. Challengers aren't just the down economy rep of today; they're the solution-selling rep of tomorrow. If you're looking to grow through solutions, you're going to need Challenger reps to do it.

If you stop and think about your best salespeople—the ones bringing in the biggest deals from the most complex customers, you can see them in this picture. Chances are they're your best Challengers.

That said, implicit in this finding is a lesson for how you might think about the less complex, more transactional parts of your business, as well. In these areas (many of them in the inside or telesales parts of your company), it probably doesn't make sense to overinvest in building

Challengers, as the data suggest that Hard Workers are more likely to win the day there. If sales success is more a matter of call volume than call quality, Hard Workers are primed to succeed. Challengers are critical in the complex world of solution selling, but they're not requisite for every part of the business.

The overall conclusion from our research is this: If you're on the journey to more of a value-based or solutions-oriented sales approach, then your ability to *challenge* customers is absolutely vital for your success going forward. It's therefore imperative to understand just what exactly makes someone a Challenger. After all, it's one thing to tell reps, "Be a Challenger!" It's another thing altogether to tell them exactly what you want them to *do*.

3

THE CHALLENGER (PART 2):

EXPORTING THE MODEL TO THE CORE

A CHALLENGER IS defined by the ability to do three things—teach, tailor, and take control—and to do all of this through the use of constructive tension.

These are the pillars of what we call the Challenger Selling Model—an approach to sales that is based on what Challengers do. It's a methodology that we've worked on with companies across a wide range of industries—companies as diverse as Talecris Biotherapeutics, PMI, Brinks, and the solutions business of Thomson Reuters—to implement within their own sales organizations. It's premised on the notion that with the right training, coaching, and sales tools, most reps—even ardent Relationship Builders—can learn to take control of the customer conversation like a Challenger.

The Challenger Selling Model is simple in theory, but complex in practice, and early adopters will attest to that. The rest of this book is dedicated to sharing proven best practices, tools, and lessons learned to help companies, commercial leaders, managers, and reps implement the Challenger Selling Model.

Before we begin this journey, it makes sense to discuss some of the fundamental principles that underlie the model and that will become themes throughout the course of this book.

Principle #1: Challengers Are Made, Not Just Born

One of the questions we often hear is whether being a Challenger is a question of nature or nurture for sales reps. In other words, are Challengers born or made? There are a few ways to answer this question.

One of the things we know from our research is that every rep in our study had traces of the Challenger "gene," it just wasn't the thing they "majored" in. But because we focused our work specifically on skills, attitudes, behaviors, and knowledge, that tell us that with the right tools, training, coaching, and reward and recognition system, you can likely equip many of your reps who minor in challenging (and maybe even those who just took a few credits in it) to act more like Challengers when they're in front of the customer. While there may be reps who won't make the transition, there are many, many more who will if you invest the time and energy to get them there.

Furthermore, the idea that Challengers are born and not made is somewhat irrelevant. While we might not be able to rewrite their DNA, if we are able to modify non–Challenger rep behavior even temporarily as they face off with customers (to "flex," as one member put it), that effort is likely time well spent. After all, we aren't aware of any sales leader who is ready to let go of all but a handful of his reps and rehire an entirely new sales force—that is, no head of sales who wants to keep his job.

Our operating principle with members has been to focus on arming them with the tools and training they need to improve their existing sales force right now. This is a worthy goal and one that the best organizations have shown great success in pursuing. There is ample evidence to suggest that Challengers can be made. We've seen this firsthand and have had tremendous success helping companies build Challengers within their own organizations.

If you are a sales rep, regardless of whether or not you are a natural Challenger, this discussion of the Challenger Sales Model contains insights that will help boost your personal effectiveness as a salesperson. While your current approach may differ from the Challenger model, don't think of these differences as insurmountable or somehow carved in stone. Understanding that these gaps exist and, more important, that you have it in your power to close them, is a critical part of the journey.

Principle #2: It's the Combination of Skills That Matters

One of the key lessons from our work is that it's the combination of the Challenger attributes—the ability to teach, tailor, take control, and do it all while leveraging constructive tension—that sets Challengers apart.

If you teach without tailoring, you come off as irrelevant. If you tailor but don't teach, you risk sounding like every other supplier. If you take control but offer no value, you risk being simply annoying. Thus the Venn diagram you see in figure 3.1. This is a graphical snapshot of what "good" looks like when it comes to rep performance. Think of this as a single snapshot of the "new high performer." Because these skills are most effective when used in combination, we strongly urge our members to avoid the temptation to "cherry-pick" when it comes to rolling out the model.

But just as nature abhors a vacuum, companies abhor duplicative investment. For this reason, we often hear commercial leaders talk about skipping elements of the model given recent initiatives. For instance, some companies wish to focus only on tailoring and taking control because they recently poured money into designing new sales collateral. While we can't dictate what companies do with the model, we are upfront with our feedback around such partial rollouts: Individual elements of the model, when invested in, can deliver performance improvements over the status quo, but for the model to really work, all elements must be invested in and developed. There are no shortcuts to fully realizing the potential performance gains that the model offers.

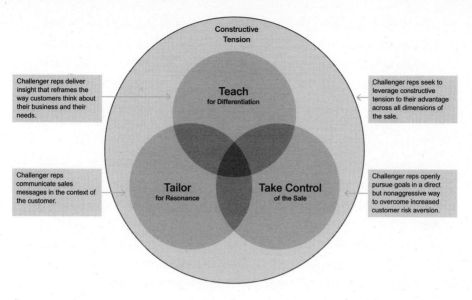

Constructive
Tension

Challenger reps deliver insight that reframes the way customers think about their business and their needs.

Teach
for Differentiation

Challenger reps seek to leverage constructive tension to their advantage across all dimensions of the sale.

Challenger reps communicate sales messages in the context of the customer.

Tailor
for Resonance

Take Control
of the Sale

Challenger reps openly pursue goals in a direct but nonaggressive way to overcome increased customer risk aversion.

Source: CEB, CEB Sales Leadership Council, 2011.

Figure 3.1. Key Skills Within the Challenger Selling Model

Principle #3: Challenging Is About Organizational Capability, Not Just Rep Skills

Many organizations assume that the migration to the Challenger Selling Model is a question only of improving individual rep skills. For the model to really work, that is emphatically not the case. This journey is actually just as much about building organizational capabilities as it is about developing individual skills.

Building a teaching capability, which we will discuss in much more detail in the following chapters, is not something that you just want your individual reps out there figuring out on their own. While it is true that some of your existing Challengers can do this effectively, an organization that leaves the teaching content up to its individual reps will be pulled in many different directions as reps promise customers solutions to myriad business issues—including many your company is not equipped to solve.

The act of delivering a teaching pitch is a skill, to be sure, but the *content* of a teaching pitch—the business issues you teach customers to value, the idea around which you reframe how the customer thinks about their business—must be scalable and repeatable, and as such, must be created by the organization (in most organizations, this is the job of marketing).

The same can be said for parts of tailoring. While there is a clear role for the individual rep on the tailoring front, namely, recognizing how to modify the teaching message for different individuals across the customer organization, the organization has an important responsibility when it comes to tailoring as well. First, organizations can leverage business intelligence and research assets to help developing Challengers better tailor their messages to each customer's industry and company context. The organization also bears the responsibility for identifying which teaching messages will resonate with which stakeholders. A one-size-fits-all teaching message is unlikely to be tenable for most suppliers, aside from those who sell in a single line of business to a highly homogeneous set of customers. Yet individual customer stakeholder segmentation at this level, again, is just as much an organizational capability as it is an individual skill.

If tailoring is half individual/half organizational, the only component of the Challenger model that can truly be called a *largely* individual skill is taking control. Here is where rep upskilling will pay significant dividends, and in chapter 7 we will explain the best way to drive this behavior into the front line. However, it is worth noting that even here, the organization has a role to play. Namely, Challenger reps armed with powerful teaching messages produced by their organizations will be in a much better position to take control of the customer conversation. As well, our recent research shows that the organization plays an important role in equipping reps to identify and properly engage with the right stakeholders on the customer side—an important part of taking control of the sale.

Principle #4: Building the Challenger Sales Force Is a Journey, Not an Overnight Trip

A big mistake we see organizations make in their Challenger efforts is assuming that change will happen instantly. Moving to a Challenger model is a commercial transformation, one that early adopters tell us takes time to get right. Precisely because the Challenger model demands changes both to organizational capabilities and to individual rep behaviors and skills, it is hard work.

Ramming through Challenger training for reps without also carefully constructing robust teaching pitches for them to deliver or arming frontline managers to reinforce the right behaviors and skills might yield a small bump in rep productivity, but two outcomes are practically guaranteed: The performance boost attained will fall well short of what it could have delivered if done properly, and more likely than not it will be perceived as the training "flavor of the month," soon to be forgotten or rejected by most reps.

Early adopters attest to the fact that moving to the Challenger Selling Model is a journey. Those who've been down this path peg the time to full adoption in terms of years, not weeks or months. Indeed, much of the upfront effort will be spent getting your own leadership team on board with the new model. The Challenger model, in other words, isn't a bolt-on software update—it's a new operating system for the commercial organization. Those looking for a quick win would be well advised to look elsewhere.

If you're ready to take your organization on this transformation journey, however, read on. The advantages that are accruing to first movers are enormous. The Challenger model offers a new and powerful way out of the solution selling morass that has had sales organizations across industries and around the world in a vise grip for years.

DOES THE CHALLENGER SELLING MODEL WORK?

Soon after we began sharing the findings from our research, we began hearing stories back from our members about how their reps were employing the principles of the Challenger Selling Model with customers—often to outstanding effect. Let's look at each of the pillars of the model in turn to give a sense of what it looks like when done well.

Teaching for Differentiation

The thing that really sets Challenger reps apart is their ability to teach customers something new and valuable about how to compete in their market. Our research on customer loyalty, which we'll discuss in depth in the next chapter, shows that this is the exact behavior that wins customers for the long term.

Teaching is all about offering customers unique perspectives on their business and communicating those perspectives with passion and precision in a way that draws the customer into the conversation. These new perspectives apply not to your products and solutions, but to how the customer can compete more effectively in their market. It's insight they can use to free up operating expenses, penetrate new markets, or reduce risk.

To see how this teaching approach works in practice, we'll give you a few examples. The first is from one of our members at an office furniture manufacturer. A senior member of the company's sales leadership team told us the story of a rep who was struggling to gain traction with a prospective customer. The customer had just built a new headquarters facility and one of their competitors had been selected to furnish the building. The company seemed to have been cut out of the business, but the rep—a brand-new hire—still felt there was an opportunity to gain a foothold in the new building before the company took delivery from their competitor. After some persistence, she landed a meeting with the company's head of real estate and facilities.

One of the key priorities for this company was to create collaborative spaces where employees could more effectively interact with one another. In looking at the architect's designs, she was able to tell him, "Well, we have robust data that indicates that collaboration doesn't happen in groups of eights. It happens in twos and threes, and when you get to seven it stops being productive. You may be building the wrong size conference rooms."

"That's great to know," responded the customer, "but the conference rooms have already been built. What can we do about that now?"

Leveraging her product knowledge, the rep explained how they could put up a movable wall down the middle of the conference rooms, creating two rooms that would fit smaller groups of three and four. Then she talked about a product the company offers that could help facilitate collaboration for them. She started from an insight, taught the customer about a problem they didn't know they had, developed interest, and changed the whole direction of the account.

Another good example comes from a global pharmaceutical company. Anybody who knows pharma knows about the arms race that the industry's big players have been locked in for years—too many reps fighting to get face time with too few doctors. In this tough sales environment, this particular company was looking to break through and become the supplier that physicians prefer to spend time with. However, customer survey data clearly indicated that in the eyes of customers, suppliers were indistinguishable from one another.

To cut through the noise, the company in question worked to arm its reps to teach physicians new insights—not about their products, but about how to improve their own effectiveness as medical practitioners. Relying on the company's wealth of knowledge on disease management, their marketing team built a series of "patient journeys" that reps could share with doctors. These journeys looked at the entire cycle of an illness, from the time symptoms appear to treatment and, finally, follow-up.

For a doctor, seeing the full life cycle of an illness can be pretty eye-opening. For example, the company knows that patients with a certain illness have an average of 2.5 exacerbations—frequently requiring a visit to the emergency room—a year. However, the family physician for these patients might never know that these emergencies occur between visits. As a consequence, they are treating the patients for a much less severe medical condition than the patients actually have. Once they learn this new information, they can change the patient's treatment to avoid or substantially reduce these exacerbations, which really improves the quality of patient care the physician can deliver. This is insight physicians value, and it's helped this particular supplier gain access to physicians in a way they never enjoyed before.

One last example. In sales these days, there's a lot of discussion about how reps can "get ahead of the RFP." This story illustrates how teaching can be used effectively not just to get ahead of an RFP, but to actually reshape an RFP in a given supplier's favor.

The story comes from a supplier of employee benefit management services who was recently informed by a longtime customer that the company had decided to put the contract for the business out to bid in an attempt to save money. Frustrated that this longtime customer was trying to pull them into a price war, the supplier told them that they weren't interested in that kind of partnership with a client, i.e., one based on price. So they told the customer that they would respectfully decline to submit a bid in response to the forthcoming RFP. But not before they made a rather unique gesture.

They told the customer that since they weren't going to be participating in the bidding process, but valued the long-term working relationship they had, they would be happy to help them think through the construction of their RFP to ensure that they were requesting the right things out of their next supplier.

Appreciative of the free consulting the supplier was offering, the customer invited them down for the day, where they spent a few hours outlining what should be in the bid. The discussions included advice along the lines of, "If any supplier tells you the following three things, they're wrong. And here's why." "If they say you need these four things, you actually don't, and here's why." "No matter what, make sure that your bid includes the following two things, and here's why." "If any company tells you those two things aren't necessary, tell them they're wrong. And here's why. They're just trying to get you to buy what they want to sell, but here's why you need to insist on these two key things."

The customer found the advice to be hugely valuable, as these were points they wouldn't have thought to consider on their own. Once the RFP was built, the supplier's account team looked at it and said, "Okay, well, if *that* is the bid you're going to put out there, then we'd like to participate since it describes exactly the kind of partnership we'd like to have with you."

This last example in particular illustrates why this teaching approach works so well. The content of the rep's teaching pitch is carefully linked to the supplier's unique capabilities. The ability of a sales rep to deliver this kind of unique insight is arguably the most powerful weapon in the Challenger's arsenal and actually the biggest driver of B2B customer loyalty. We'll focus on building this kind of teaching capability in chapters 4 and 5.

Tailoring for Resonance

While teaching is above all others the defining attribute of being a Challenger, the ability to tailor the teaching message to different types of customers—as well as to different individuals within the customer organization—is what makes the teaching pitch resonate and stick with the customer.

Tailoring relies on the rep's knowledge of the specific business priorities of whomever he or she is talking to—the specific outcomes that particular person values most, the results they're on the hook to deliver for their company, and the various economic drivers most likely to affect those outcomes.

If a Challenger rep is sitting across the table from a head of marketing, he understands how to craft his message to resonate with her specific priorities. And if he's meeting with someone in operations, he knows how to modify the message accordingly. But this isn't just a measure of business acumen, it's a measure of agility—the rep's ability to tailor the story to the individual stakeholder's business environment. What specifically do they care about? How is their performance measured? How do they fit into the overall customer organization?

An example that demonstrates the power of effective tailoring comes from our member at a business services provider. Two of their reps had been jointly working one account for approximately six months, building rapport with the business leaders across the organization, all the while preparing for a big proposal presentation to the company's CEO and management team. After multiple meetings and presentations, the reps homed in on what they thought was most needed by the customer— an outsourcing solution that would deliver cost savings to the business.

But just a week before they were about to present to the CEO and his team, the reps attended their own company's annual sales meeting, which had focused on building Challenger skills across the sales organization. At the session on tailoring, the reps realized that they hadn't fully investigated the personal motivations and business objectives of the customer's CEO and were potentially unprepared to make their best pitch at the upcoming meeting.

They called a last-minute meeting with some of the key stakeholders in the customer organization to better understand the personal goals and objectives of the CEO—all in an attempt to see if there was some insight they could bring to the table that would personally appeal to him. What they learned in this meeting proved invaluable. They found out that the CEO was extremely focused on the poor customer satisfaction scores the company had recently received. And they learned that the CEO was himself a technology junkie.

Instead of going into the meeting with the cost savings–focused pitch they had already prepared, they switched gears and focused the conversation on ways in which the solution they were proposing not only would cut costs but could at the same time improve customer satisfaction and issue resolution response time by leveraging new technologies the supplier had recently developed. What's more, the technology would allow everyone from the CEO down to line managers to get real-time visibility into customer service issues and issue resolution response times.

The CEO immediately sat up and listened with rapt attention to the sales pitch. What was to be a standard review of a supplier proposal turned into a surprising discussion of one of the CEO's hot-button issues. At the end of the presentation, the CEO thanked the reps for shedding new light on a persistent business problem and demonstrating capabilities that he didn't realize the supplier had. While the competitors stuck to their standard proposals, this supplier won the business by tailoring their message to what the CEO cared about most. In a time when consensus is more important than ever to get the deal done, it's no surprise that the rep who wins in this environment is the one who can effectively tailor the message to a wide range of customer stakeholders in order to build that consensus. This is a topic we're going to explore in a lot more depth in chapter 6.

Taking Control of the Sale

The final characteristic that sets Challenger reps apart is their ability to assert and maintain control over the sale. Now, before we go any further, it's important to note that being assertive does not mean being aggressive or, worse still, annoying or abusive. This is all about the reps' willingness and ability to stand their ground when the customer pushes back.

A Challenger's assertiveness takes two forms. First, Challengers are able to assert control over the discussion of pricing and money more generally. The Challenger rep doesn't give in to the request for a 10 percent discount, but brings the conversation back to the overall solution—pushing for agreement on value, rather than price. Second, Challengers are also able to challenge customers' thinking and pressure the customer's decision-making cycle—both to reach a decision more quickly as well as to overcome that "indecision inertia" that can cause deals to stall indefinitely.

In fact, if you think about it, if a key to a Challenger rep's success is teaching—or reframing how that customer sees their world—then the rep is going to have to be willing to get a little scuffed up in the process. Just as you can't be an effective teacher if you're not going to push your students, you can't be an effective Challenger if you're not going to push your customers. This approach is so important today with customer risk aversion as high as it is. It's funny, sales leaders often lament that core-performing reps fall into their comfort zone when selling, but arguably the bigger problem is that customers often fall into their comfort zone when it comes to buying. And that's what the Challenger rep does—she moves customers out of their comfort zone by showing them their world in a different light. The key, of course, is to do this with control, diplomacy, and empathy.

As one of our longtime members, the former CSO of one of the world's largest chemical manufacturers, explains, "In practice, asserting control can take many forms. In essence, it means that the sales professional takes the lead in the customer discussion with a specific end in mind." While the entire toolkit for taking control is both large and complex, there are many simple tools that can be applied with power.

"Discussions over price—price increases or requests for price decreases—are very high-value areas for the sales professional to take control of," he says. "When the topic of price comes up, a powerful technique is for the sales professional to shift the discussion from price to value. The value of the current offering is a great place to start this dialogue. During the course of such a discussion, it is useful to get the customer to rank the elements of the offering in order of importance. This sometimes enables the customer to see the offering in a different light; these new insights are very useful to both the sales professional and the customer as they think about value."

He told us the story of one of his sales reps, who was in a situation where he had to let a longtime customer know about a price increase—one that was not only substantial, but also out of sync with the economy. None of the customer's other suppliers were raising prices, but the raw material for the supplier's product had gone up so much that it dictated the need.

At the same time, years before, that same customer had requested that the product be shipped in an expensive, nonstandard package. Over time, the cost of this package had substantially reduced the profitability of the business for the supplier. During the discussion of the price increase, the sales professional asked the customer to rank the various features of the supplier's offering. The expensive custom packaging didn't rank in the top three. As a consequence, the supplier and the sales professional agreed to a lower price increase and a shift to standard packaging. The change in packaging improved profitability more than the price increase itself. "This was a great outcome," he said, "using a relatively simple device to assert control in a price discussion to deliver a win for both parties."

A ROAD MAP FOR THE REST OF THIS BOOK

What's the best path to building Challenger reps? Here is how we'll tackle this question in the following chapters:

- In chapters 4 and 5, we'll look at the notion of teaching. We'll address the questions of why teaching works and what your reps should be teaching in the first place—as well as what the content of their "teaching pitch" should look like. Much of this chapter will center on the critical role that the organization—in most companies, marketing—plays in identifying "customer-worthy insights" that lead to a supplier's unique capabilities.
- In chapter 6, we'll look at tailoring. We'll take a deep dive into why tailoring is an effective approach in today's sales environment and look at what the best sales organizations do to equip their reps to tailor—in other words, get them to adapt their sales approach and message to specific individuals across the customer organization. A critical part of the tailoring story is the shift we discussed in chapter 1 toward consensus buying within customer organizations. We'll spend some time unpacking this trend in more detail in chapter 6.
- In chapter 7, we'll dig deep into the area of taking control and discuss techniques for getting reps to increase their

assertiveness without becoming aggressive. As mentioned before, taking control is an easily misunderstood element of the Challenger Selling Model. Poorly applied, it will do more harm than good, but correctly applied, it can be the difference between a decision and "no decision." In a world where the customer's status quo is really your worst enemy, and customers are so increasingly risk-averse, the ability to take control can be a game-changer for your sales reps.

- In chapter 8, we will look at the critical role of the frontline sales manager in building Challengers across the sales force. Specifically, we'll look at the issue of coaching—something most sales organizations continue to neglect. This is an area of deep expertise for us and one where we have some counterintuitive data and powerful best practices to share with you. The story doesn't end with coaching, however. In some recent work we've completed, we've found that high-performing sales managers also possess a unique ability to innovate at the deal level with their reps. If coaching is about imparting skills known to drive sales success, sales innovation is about moving individual deals forward in a purposeful manner. They're different skills, but both are hugely important in an organization seeking to make a shift to the Challenger model.

- In chapter 9, we'll offer some additional words of guidance to leaders who are seeking to transform their commercial organizations into Challenger organizations. If you're going to embark on this journey of building Challengers, how do you design the change effort so that it leads to real, long-term change and not just the next "flavor of the month" upskilling effort?

- Lastly, in the afterword, we'll look at the notion of challenging beyond the world of sales. The Challenger model is one that, we believe, is a business concept, not just a sales concept, and is one that we've seen effectively employed in a variety of corporate settings—from IT to HR to finance, legal, and strategy—and we'll discuss this in more detail in this closing section of the book.

TEACHING FOR DIFFERENTIATION (PART 1):
WHY INSIGHT MATTERS

OVER THE LAST fifteen years, most sales training has centered on a core principle: The shortest path to sales success is a deep understanding of customers' needs. If you're going to sell "solutions," the thinking goes, you've got to first "discover" your customers' most pressing points of pain and then build a tight connection between what's keeping them up at night and what you're seeking to sell.

Not surprisingly, then, sales leaders have spent millions of dollars and untold hours training reps to ask better questions. Lots of them. Probing questions. Financial questions. Hypothetical questions. Open-ended questions. Follow-up questions. All designed to figure out as deeply as possible customers' "top three strategic objectives for the coming year," or "the two things they've got to get right this quarter," or—better still—their current "burning platforms."

The idea being, if we just dig deep enough to find "the story behind the story," we'll eventually get to a place where customers are so forthcoming about what they truly need that right there on the spot we can craft a highly targeted offer that provides the perfect "solution" to their problem. A solution so perfectly aligned with their needs that they have no choice but to buy it—no matter what the cost.

It sounds great on paper, but this approach suffers one major problem: It doesn't work nearly as well today as it used to. Certainly it no longer warrants the massive training investments poured into improving reps' discovery skills. And that's not just because improving reps' ability to ask good questions proves colossally difficult—especially among core-performing reps—but, much more important, because this approach is based on a deeply flawed assumption: that customers actually *know* what they need in the first place. That customer needs are simply there waiting to be unlocked, either willingly or begrudgingly, through the mastery of our interrogative technique.

But what if customers truly don't know what they need? What if customers' single greatest need—ironically—is to *figure out* exactly what they need?

If this were true, rather than *asking* customers what they need, the better sales technique might in fact be to *tell* customers what they need. And that's exactly what Challengers do. When you get down to it, Challengers aren't so much world-class investigators as they are world-class teachers. They win not by understanding their customers' world as well as the customers know it themselves, but by actually knowing their customers' world *better* than their customers know it themselves, teaching them what they don't know but should.

Across the next two chapters we dive deep into the Challenger's ability to teach—arguably the first among equals across the three central Challenger competencies. A critical part of our teaching story will be a close, concrete look at what teaching is and is not. What it looks like and sounds like, how it works, and how to ensure we get paid when it's done right. And along the way, we'll address tough questions with some surprising answers. Things like:

- How exactly is a "teaching" conversation all that different from a traditional sales conversation?
- What kind of collateral do I need to teach effectively?
- How much of this is truly a matter of individual skill versus organizational capability?
- What's the role of marketing in getting this right?

And perhaps most important:

- Do customers really want to be taught in the first place?

Let's start with the last question first. That's really where the rubber hits the road in any sales approach: with the customer. And in the case of the Challenger approach, this is the question we hear most often. After all, it seems on the surface rather arrogant to simply show up and declare to the customer, "Hello, I'm here to teach you!"

But that's exactly what we're saying. Perhaps not in those words per se—in fact, almost certainly not in those words. But still, after four years of extensive customer research, what we emphatically know to be true is that that's *exactly* what customers are looking for more than anything else in a supplier.

IT'S NOT WHAT YOU SELL, IT'S HOW YOU SELL

Beginning long before the global economy went off a cliff in 2008 and continuing right through the ensuing downturn, CEB had surveyed well over 5,000 individuals at members' clients' customer organizations—everyone from business owners and C-suite executives to end users, purchase influencers, procurement officers, and even third-party consultants—in order to determine what exactly they're looking for in a business-to-business supplier.

Specifically, across roughly fifty questions we asked each respondent to rank the named supplier (i.e., our client organization) versus similar suppliers in terms of various attributes of their products, brand, service, and price-to-value ratio. We asked about all the typical reasons why someone might choose one supplier over another—things like product performance, product features, brand recognition, service response times. In addition, we asked those same individuals a number of questions about the sales experience itself—what it's actually like to buy from the named supplier relative to their competitors. Finally, we asked each respondent three specific questions to gauge their level of loyalty to that supplier: "On a scale from one to seven, how willing are you to:

- keep buying from this particular supplier;
- buy even more from this supplier going forward;
- advocate on this supplier's behalf across your organization?"

We weren't asking about a customer's general level of happiness, or satisfaction, or even likelihood to buy—all of which we've found to have little impact on B2B customer loyalty—but rather about their willingness to join that supplier on a "solutions journey." Across years of loyalty research, we've found that the combination of these three questions better predicts deeper customer relationships and, ultimately, commercial growth than any other loyalty metric we've tested.

When we put all of that information together—tens of thousands of data points—and then run it through extensive analysis, it allows us to determine, of all the ways to outperform the competition, what the most important factors actually *are* driving up customer loyalty.

The answer is not only fascinating but so unexpected for most sales and marketing executives that the results have landed in more boardroom-level conversations than any other piece of research we've ever conducted (see figure 4.1).

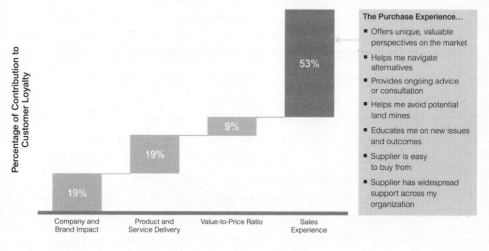

Source: CEB, CEB Sales Leadership Council, 2011.

Figure 4.1. Representative Drivers of Customer Loyalty

The first thing you find when you look at the analysis is a definitive impact on loyalty from brand, product, and service. When you combine these factors you find that 38 percent of customer loyalty is attributable to your ability to outperform the competition in these areas. Selling a well-branded, highly differentiated product, supported by higher-than-industry-average service will undoubtedly get you more loyalty. If you're way behind the competition in any of these three categories, that's probably where you want to start.

That said, many executives look at these results with genuine surprise. They expect these factors to account for much more, maybe 70, 80, or even 90 percent of customer loyalty. After all, if they can't win loyalty off their superior brand, product, and service, well then, what else is there?

But the reason for their surprisingly low impact stems largely from a common trend captured perfectly in a story told to us recently by the global head of marketing at one of the world's top financial services firms. When she saw this data, she said, "Four years ago, our company was sitting at only 65 percent customer satisfaction due to a long trend of generally poor customer service across our entire industry. Seeing this problem as a real growth opportunity, across the next three years we set about analyzing and improving service across every major customer touchpoint, investing millions of dollars and countless hours along the way. And the results were phenomenal! At the end of three years, we had increased customer satisfaction from 65 percent to 95 percent." Sounds fantastic, doesn't it?

"But," she continued, "there was only one problem. In those same three years, our two biggest competitors did the exact same thing. They invested roughly the same amount of money and achieved more or less the exact same result. So here we are, four years later, and our entire industry sits at 96 percent customer satisfaction. Don't get me wrong, that's great, but as a result we've seen absolutely no commercial benefit from all that expense. Satisfied customers leave us every day, because they know they'll be treated equally well somewhere else."

Now, is it fair to say that this company had to invest that kind of time and money simply to stay in the game? Absolutely. Had they not, they'd just as likely be out of business today. But the lesson is still maddeningly familiar. We pour millions of dollars into brand, product, and service seeking growth, and really only get status quo. Our customers are more satisfied, but they're not necessarily any more loyal.

So what's happening here? To find out, we went out and discussed these findings with some of the customers who had completed the survey and heard something that might surprise you. In light of the results—the relatively low impact on loyalty of brand, product, and service—we expected at least *some* of these customers to express real dissatisfaction with the supplier in questions across these three categories. But that's not what we heard at all. In fact, it was just the opposite. They *loved* the product! The brand was *world-class*! The service was *fantastic*! But if that was the case, then why in the world were the loyalty scores for these attributes so low?

The answer lay in what these customers would often say next. "Sure! They've got a *great* product! It performs exactly like they said it would! But the competition's got a great product too!" Or, "Their brand is *world-class*! *Everyone* knows their brand! But the competition's got a world-class brand too!" Or, "Their service is *fantastic*! In fact, I'd put them right up there with the competition!" Sound familiar?

Over and over we found that customers, generally speaking, see significantly less difference between us and the competition than we do ourselves. It's not that they think most suppliers are particularly *bad* on brand, product, or service. It's just that they don't think they're particularly *different*. So while we spend much of our time emphasizing subtle differences, customers tend to focus first on the general similarities.

Does this mean you should stop investing in brand, product, and service? Certainly not! It's all still hugely important. But—at least in the B2B world—the investments we make in brand building, product development, and improved customer service are not the *final* step to winning customer loyalty, but the *first*. It's the price of entry to gaining customer loyalty at all.

In fact, after they've had a chance to wrap their heads around this finding for a while, sales and marketing executives tend to agree, as they see it every single day in their own business. However, in many cases, their natural inclination across the last several years, at least, is to explain away the low impact on loyalty from brand, product, and service as a natural by-product of customers' intense focus on reducing costs. Sure, customers are loyal, they'd argue. They're just loyal to whoever's got the lowest price.

But it turns out, that's not the case either. Only 9 percent of customer loyalty is attributable to a supplier's ability to outperform the competition on price-to-value ratio. Yes, you might be cheaper than the competition, but in the eyes of your customer, you likely provide less value as well. So your lower price may get you the deal, but it almost certainly won't get you much loyalty.

If your customer is dead set on buying the cheapest option today, then chances are pretty good they'll be dead set on buying the cheapest option tomorrow as well. And that may or may not be you. After all, there's usually little stopping your competition from discounting their way to a win. In that game, loyalty is essentially irrelevant, as customers aren't looking for a partner, they're looking for a *bargain*. And that's not what this story is all about. This is a story about a customer's willingness not only to keep buying from you, but to buy even more over time and to advocate on your behalf. And if that's your goal, price is simply a bad way to get there. Unless your lower prices come with significantly higher perceived value than the competition, today's discounts won't get you tomorrow's business.

So if only 38 percent of customer loyalty is attributable to your ability to outperform the competition on brand, product, and service, and 9 percent of loyalty is attributable to your ability to outperform the competition on price-to-value ratio, then what about the other 53 percent? What else is there?

Well, to understand the answer, let's go back to those customer conversations we mentioned a moment ago. What we typically heard from customers, after they told us how little difference they saw between one supplier and another in terms of brand, product, and service, is that they saw huge differences in the sales experience itself—the actual sales conversations they had with suppliers on an ongoing basis.

Customers were painfully blunt on this point. Some reps, they said, would so thoroughly waste their time that at the end of the sales call they felt as though they'd just been robbed of an hour of their lives—an hour they will never get back. And frankly, it didn't matter how good the rep's presentation skills might be. It just wasn't worth it to have to sit and listen to an excited explanation of how the new and improved Model XPJ178 could run three seconds faster while using less energy and requiring less maintenance, "saving you time and money for the more important things!" Who cares?!?! Do I want to save time and money? Of course I do! Do I think that three seconds justifies a 5 percent price premium? Probably not.

On the other hand, those same customers told us that *other* reps would take the time to provide information so interesting and valuable that—in the words of Neil Rackham—the customer would have been willing to *pay for the conversation itself.* In other words, while customers found some suppliers to be horrible in the sales experience, they found others to be invaluable. Even suppliers that appeared similar in every other way on paper performed all over the map when it came to the sales experience. And that difference, it turns out, has a huge impact on customer loyalty.

That's the real bombshell finding of this work. Loyalty isn't won in product development centers, in advertisements, or on toll-free help lines: Loyalty is won out in the field, in the trenches, during the sales call. It's the result of the conversations our reps are having with customers every single day. The entire remainder of customer loyalty—all 53 percent—is attributable to your ability to outperform the competition in the sales experience itself. Over half of customer loyalty is a result not of *what* you sell, but *how* you sell. As important as it is to have great products, brand, and service, it's all for naught if your reps can't execute out in the field.

That said, it's one thing to say that the sales experience is hugely important for customer loyalty, but another thing altogether to understand how. After all, remember, customers were very specific here. Some of these interactions are desperately painful, others incredibly valuable. So what exactly needs to happen during the sales experience in order to generate such an impact on customer loyalty?

Well, this is where the story really gets interesting, because when you crack open the data inside the sales experience category, what you find is the exact same Challenger story, only this time from the customer's perspective.

THE POWER OF INSIGHT

Of the fifty or so attributes we tested in our loyalty survey, seventeen of them fell into the sales experience category, each reflecting at least a marginally positive impact on customer loyalty. They included things like, "Demonstrates a high level of professionalism," "Adjusts to our unique needs and specifications," "Portrays a realistic picture of costs," and "Matches communications to my preferences." However, when we ranked the list according to impact, we found seven in particular that rose way above the others in terms of importance:

- Rep offers unique and valuable perspectives on the market.
- Rep helps me navigate alternatives.
- Rep provides ongoing advice or consultation.
- Rep helps me avoid potential land mines.
- Rep educates me on new issues and outcomes.
- Supplier is easy to buy from.
- Supplier has widespread support across my organization.

Now, if we start at the bottom of that list and work up, the first thing we find is statistical corroboration for what we all know to be true—and something we'll discuss in more depth in chapter 6. The need for consensus across customer stakeholders has gone way up. Senior decision makers inside the customer are no longer willing to go out on a limb for any supplier or any solution, unless that deal has the support of his or her team.

It's a logical, if frustrating, outcome of the larger, more expensive, more disruptive solutions suppliers are seeking to sell. When the stakes are higher, you can't just claw your way to the corner office to get the deal done. You've got to build a network of advocacy along the way or risk losing the deal altogether due to weak support across the organization.

Likewise, customers place a great deal of importance on a smooth, uncomplicated purchase. No one wants to work with a supplier that makes any purchase more complicated than it has to be—especially a solutions purchase. Nothing slows down a deal faster than reps who have to constantly "check with their manager," or "run it through Legal," or "see if Finance will be willing to do that." Don't make your customers work so hard to spend their money!

There's something else about this list that really jumps out. Take another look at the top five attributes listed there—the key characteristics defining a world-class sales experience:

- Rep offers unique and valuable perspectives on the market.
- Rep helps me navigate alternatives.
- Rep provides ongoing advice or consultation.
- Rep helps me avoid potential land mines.
- Rep educates me on new issues and outcomes.

Each of these attributes speaks directly to an urgent need of the customer not to *buy* something, but to *learn* something. They're looking to suppliers to help them identify new opportunities to cut costs, increase revenue, penetrate new markets, and mitigate risk in ways they themselves have not yet recognized. Essentially this is the customer—or 5,000 of them at least, all over the world—saying rather emphatically, "Stop wasting my time. Challenge me. Teach me something new."

It's a powerful conclusion that runs contrary to years of thought and training in B2B sales. Sure, a supplier has to have great products, brand, and service. But from the customer's perspective, most already do. After all, if that weren't the case, they probably wouldn't be speaking with that supplier in the first place. Instead, what sets the best suppliers apart is not the quality of their products, but the *value of their insight*—new ideas to help customers either make money or save money in ways they didn't even know were possible.

In this sense, customer loyalty is much less about what you sell and much more about how you sell. The best companies don't win through the quality of the products they sell, but through the quality of the insight they deliver as part of the sale itself. The battle for customer loyalty is won or lost long before a thing ever gets sold. And the best reps win that battle not by "discovering" what customers already know they need, but by teaching them a new way of thinking altogether.

Customers are very clear on this point. They place much greater value on reps' teaching skills than on their discovery skills. To go back to the data for a moment, much farther down the list within the sales experience is, "The rep excels in diagnosing our specific needs." The ability to diagnose needs scores much lower because, frankly, it's just not as valuable to the customer. Sure, it's great if a rep knows my needs as well as I do and can ask great questions to uncover those needs as quickly as possible. But what I really need is a rep who knows my needs *better* than I do—one who can challenge me to think differently about my business altogether. And to do that, great questions aren't enough. You've got to have great *insights*.

And by the way, for those selling a commodity, this is all the more applicable. There's no question that winning customer loyalty when you can't differentiate yourself on product, brand, or price is difficult at best. But these findings provide the best possible path for doing just that. As a head of sales at a global chemical company put it to us, "Sure, you and I may both sell five-gallon buckets of unbranded axle grease at the same price. But if I can sell my five-gallon bucket of unbranded axle grease better than you can sell your five-gallon bucket of unbranded axle grease—well, then I'm going to win. And the way I do that is by helping the customer think differently about their business." And he's right. After all, if he's not, then there's really nothing left other than price itself as the basis for differentiation. And in that case, why have a sales force at all? Put that unbranded axle grease online and sell it through your Web site. It's a lot cheaper that way.

So where does that leave us? In this world—where quality insight trumps all else—it's no wonder, then, that Challengers win. Insight is all about teaching customers new ways of thinking, pushing them to rethink their current perspectives and approaches. And that's exactly what Challengers do. They teach customers new perspectives, specifically tailored to their most pressing business needs, in a compelling and assertive enough manner to ensure that the message not only resonates, but actually drives action. After all, if you don't change the way a customer thinks—and, ultimately, *acts*—then you haven't really taught them anything to begin with. At least nothing worth doing anything about. And where's the value in that?

NOT JUST ANY TEACHING. *COMMERCIAL* TEACHING

Still, as important as teaching is, it is not enough to simply build a team of Challenger reps and tell them, "Go forth and teach!" That may be good for customers, but not necessarily good for business. Here's how the global head of sales at a large enterprise software company put it to us: "What happens," he asked, "if my rep goes out, teaches a customer something completely new and compelling about their business, gets them all excited to take action, and that customer then takes that insight, puts it out to bid, and my competitor wins the deal? In that case, it doesn't feel like I've really won anything."

And he's right, you haven't. All you've really done is provide free consulting. Sure, you've given the customer exactly what they want, but in the process you've actually given your competitor exactly what *they* want too—your business. And that is truly a bad place to be.

It's one thing to challenge customers with new ideas, and another thing altogether to ensure you get paid for it. Even the world's best Challengers can't win if they're teaching customers to value capabilities they can't competitively provide. So how do we ensure that our teaching efforts actually lead to more business for us and not the competition? Well, to do that, we find that your teaching efforts have to meet some very specific criteria.

We call this approach Commercial Teaching. A bit unimaginative, perhaps, but we like the name nonetheless because it perfectly captures what Challengers ultimately must do: teach customers something new and valuable about their business—which is what they want—in a way that reliably leads to commercial wins for us—which of course is what we want. It sounds a bit like jujitsu, but it's actually pretty straightforward; it's just not necessarily easy. Commercial Teaching has four key rules:

1. Lead to your unique strengths.
2. Challenge customers' assumptions.
3. Catalyze action.
4. Scale across customers.

As we work through these rules, you'll find that they are as much about building an organizational capability as they are about developing an individual skill, a key lesson of the Challenger selling model we discussed in the previous chapter. This approach is about much more than simply building Challengers; it's about broad, long-term commercial transformation. More on that shortly. For now, let's review the four rules of Commercial Teaching.

Commercial Teaching Rule #1: Lead to Your Unique Strengths

First and foremost, commercial teaching must tie directly back to some capability where you outperform your competitors. If what you're teaching inevitably leads back to what you do better than anyone else, then you're in a much better position when it comes to winning the business.

We often put it like this: The sweet spot of customer loyalty is outperforming your competitors on those things you've taught your customers are important. Yes, you've got to get a customer thinking about new opportunities to save or make money—opportunities that move them to take action. But you've only really succeeded when the customer asks, "Wow, how can I make that happen?" and you're able to say, "Well, let me show you how we're better able to help you make that happen than anyone else." That's the magical moment. You've shared new, relevant insight—which is what customers are looking for—but at the same time, you've tied that insight to your unique solution. You've taught your customer not just to want help but to want *your* help.

There are two important caveats, however, to doing this well. First, in order for this approach to work, you've got to make sure that you actually *can* help. From the customer's perspective, there's nothing more frustrating than a supplier that teaches them a new and compelling way to save or make money, but then can't actually do anything about it. One head of sales we work with refers to this as "teaching your customer into the desert." You leave them troubled by a new problem they never knew they had and with no real way of doing anything about it. Yes, customers want insight on how they could operate more productively, but insight they can't do anything about actually makes things worse, not better. Then you really *have* given them something to keep them up at night!

Second, and this is the big caveat, in order to ensure that your teaching efforts ultimately lead to your unique strengths, you actually have to know what your unique strengths *are*. Sure, it sounds obvious. But we have been consistently surprised by the number of executives who struggle mightily on this issue. Here's how one head of marketing at a well-known manufacturing company put it: "If I polled a hundred reps on our core value proposition, I'd get *at least* a hundred different answers." We hear this all the time, usually coupled with a slow shake of the head and a rueful sigh; it's one of those age-old truths of sales and marketing.

Yet notice that this executive's lament really captures only part of the problem. Yes, it's hard enough to get reps to agree on a broad description of what the company does well. But ask those same reps what the company actually does *better* than the competition, and instead of a hundred different answers you're just as likely to get none at all. At best you might hear something like, "Yeah, the competition can do something like that too, but we do it so much *better*!" Or even more common: "Sure, you could go with the other guy, but keep in mind we've been in this business longer than anyone else. We've been serving leading companies for over fifty years with innovative solutions backed by a deep commitment to product quality and a laser-like focus on serving customers." Blah, blah, blah. As if your main competitor didn't have a "laser-like" focus on customers either. Of course they do!

How is a customer supposed to choose between two suppliers that are more or less undifferentiated? It's actually rather simple: They choose the cheapest supplier. Who wouldn't? In today's world, *everyone* is "innovative," "solutions-oriented," "customer-focused," and—of course— "green," so why pay more for it?

In a recent survey of B2B customers, CEB found only 35 percent of companies able to establish themselves as truly preferred over the competition. And still more troubling, even among preferred companies, when we tested the impact of each of the benefits they believed to be unique, we found that customers perceived only *half* of them to be actually relevant to their needs. And among those, customers told us that most weren't delivered consistently enough to actually influence their preference. When you put it all together, only 14 percent of companies' so-called unique benefits were perceived by customers as both unique and beneficial! And as you might imagine, being "innovative," "customer-focused," and "green" were not among them. When it comes to differentiation, your customers hold you to a much higher standard.

It's no wonder, then, that reps continually revert to price. It's not just that they struggle to articulate the value of their solution; they struggle to articulate the *unique* value of their solution. And this, it turns out, is the hardest part of commercial teaching: understanding and agreeing on what it is that your company does *better* than anyone else. It requires a very deep understanding of who you are and what you do. Much of CEB's work across the last several years has aimed at providing members the tools to figure this out—everything from step-by-step self-guided exercises, to facilitated leadership workshops, to customer survey builders, to actual customer diagnostics.

But no matter how you go about addressing it, all of this work ultimately boils down to a single question you must answer. We sometimes refer to it as the "Deb Oler question," named after Debra Oler, vice president and general manager of Grainger Brand at W. W. Grainger, Inc. As Deb puts it, "Why should our customers buy from us over anyone else?" That's it. It's disarmingly simple. But that one question can take your entire commercial leadership team to a very dark place as you realize it's much harder to answer than you might have thought. In fact, most companies can't answer it, at least not in a way that's compelling to customers (again, being "innovative," "customer-focused," and "solutions-oriented" doesn't count). And for the few companies that can answer it, even fewer still would find agreement on that answer across their entire sales force.

So where does that leave us? Well, first and foremost, it means that if you're going to build Challenger reps to teach customers something new about their business, you've likely got some work to do in your own business first. Unless you can ultimately connect the insights you teach your customers back to capabilities only you can offer, you're much more likely providing free consulting than Commercial Teaching. That's a dangerous place to be unless you happen to also be the lowest-cost provider in that market (which is improbable since lowest-cost providers, by definition, can't afford the added cost of teaching customers).

Commercial Teaching Rule #2: Challenge Customers' Assumptions

If the first rule of Commercial Teaching is all about the connection between insight and supplier, the second is about the connection between insight and customer.

It feels like an obvious point, but we'll say it anyway. Definitionally, whatever you teach your customers has to actually *teach* them something. It has to challenge their assumptions and speak directly to their world in ways they haven't thought of or fully appreciated before. The word we like to use here is "reframe." What data, information, or insight can you put in front of your customer that reframes the way they think about their business—how they operate or even how they compete? That's what your customers are really looking for. Remember what we saw in our customer survey?

- Rep offers unique and valuable perspectives on the market.
- Rep helps me navigate alternatives.
- Rep provides ongoing advice or consultation.
- Rep helps me avoid potential land mines.
- Rep educates me on new issues and outcomes.

There's nothing on that list about "confirmation" or "validation." Yes, customers appreciate it if you can confirm what they already know to be true; there's value there to be sure. But there's vastly greater value in insight that changes or builds on what they know in ways they couldn't have discovered on their own.

That kind of insight is not necessarily easy to achieve. You have to know your customers' business better than they know it themselves—at least that part of their business that speaks to your capabilities. It sounds like an impossibly high bar but the reality is that most suppliers actually *do* understand their customers' business better than customers do themselves—when viewed specifically through the lens of that supplier's capabilities. A company that sells printers to hospitals, for example, may not know more about health care than the hospital administrators they sell to, but they certainly know more about information management in a hospital setting. A company that sells consumer packaged goods probably knows more about how and why consumers buy groceries than most of the retailers they sell to.

Wherever the insight comes from, you'll know if you've actually reframed your customer's thinking based on their reaction. And this is where some reps really fall into a trap. Ironically, if your customer reacts to your sales pitch with something like, "Yes, I totally agree! That's *exactly* what's keeping me up at night!" well, then you've actually failed. That may feel counterintuitive, but it's true nonetheless. Sure, you've found an issue or insight that *resonates*, but it doesn't *reframe*. You haven't actually taught them anything. This is exactly where we see Relationship Builders struggle all the time. They return from a sales call excited about the "connection" they established with a customer because they "nailed the issue match." "It was like I was reading his mind! Everything I put on the table was something he was focused on!" But then they're surprised when that customer hasn't returned their calls two weeks later. They assume that their successful diagnosis of the customer's needs was sufficient to win the business. But that's not the case. Rapport and reframe are not the same thing. Just because you "get" the customer's business doesn't mean you automatically *get* the customer's business. Not by a long shot.

Challenger reps, on the other hand, are looking for a different customer reaction altogether. Rather than, "Yes, I totally agree!" they know they're on the right track when they hear their customer say, "Huh, I never thought of it that way before." The best indicator of a successful reframe, in other words, isn't excited agreement but thoughtful reflection. You've just shown your customer a different way to think about their business—perhaps a land mine they'd overlooked, a trend they underappreciated, or an alternative they'd prematurely dismissed—and now you've got them curious. They're wondering, "What exactly does this mean for my business?" or even better, "What *else* don't I know?"

This is the pivot point of any effective Commercial Teaching conversation. When your customer says, "Huh, I never thought about it that way before," they're clearly telling you they're engaged, maybe even a little unsettled. And as customers themselves have told us, that's exactly what they were hoping for when they sat down with you in the first place. That's when the conversation itself becomes something worth paying for.

Still, just because we've helped them *see* things differently doesn't mean we've necessarily persuaded them to *do* things differently. That's next—and it's just as important.

Commercial Teaching Rule #3: Catalyze Action

In a world of limited resources and competing priorities, it's not enough to change the way customers think. You've ultimately got to get them to act. We often joke about the customer who responds to your reframe with, "Huh, I never thought about it that way before! . . . I wonder what's for lunch . . ." Like Doug, the dog in the movie *Up* who becomes completely distracted every time he sees a squirrel, customers easily lose focus. So if you want them to take action, you'll need to build a compelling business case for why action matters in the first place.

This is well-trodden ground. For most suppliers, the move to "solutions" is grounded in an effort to justify premium prices for bundled products and services. As a result, they've invested huge amounts of time and money in a wide range of tools designed to help customers calculate the "ROI" or "total cost of ownership" of their offerings—usually accompanied by sales reps' enthusiastic assurances of the "lifetime value" of their products. "Yes, we might cost a little more up front, but look at what you can save over the next four years! Our solution practically pays for itself!" Unless you can convince your customers they'll get incremental value for that premium price, your solution strategy is doomed to fail.

In a Commercial Teaching approach, this is exactly where we find the biggest difference between companies who *believe* they do this well and those who *actually* do this well. That's because a well-executed teaching conversation isn't about the supplier's solution at all—at least not initially. It's about the customer's business, laying out an alternative means to either save money or make money they'd previously overlooked. In a conversation like that, traditional ROI calculations prove useless because they're focused on the wrong thing.

Nearly every ROI calculator we know of is built to help customers calculate the return on buying the supplier's solution. But before you convince customers to take that action, you first have to show them why the insight you just shared with them merits any action at all, especially when that insight competes directly with conventional wisdom. To that end, the best ROI calculators in a teaching approach have nothing to do with your solution at all. Rather, they help customers calculate the costs they're incurring or the returns they're forgoing by failing to act on the opportunity you've just taught them they've overlooked.

If you're going to build an ROI calculator, make sure it calculates the return on pursuing the reframe, not purchasing your products. Before they buy anything, customers first need to understand what's in it for them to fix their problem.

Commercial Teaching Rule #4: Scale Across Customers

Done well, Commercial Teaching is much more than simply an effective sales technique. It's a powerful commercial strategy. To be sure, it absolutely works well at the individual deal level, as Challenger reps opportunistically uncover occasions to teach customers fresh insights tailored to their specific context. However, there are a number of important reasons why the approach is unquestionably more effective when deployed segment by segment rather than customer by customer.

From a tactical perspective, it's not realistic or fair to expect your reps to understand their customers' business better than they do themselves without at least some organizational support. Your core performers will struggle mightily with that task no matter how much you train them—especially if they work across a diverse customer base.

But imagine if you could provide those same reps with a manageably small set of well-scripted insights along with two or three easy-to-remember diagnostic questions designed to map the right insight to the right customer. Then they'd be in a much better position to teach. It would significantly shift the burden of effective needs diagnosis away from frontline sales reps and back into the organization, where you've got both the depth of skill and the breadth of insight necessary to figure it out in advance.

For this approach to truly work, you need a small number of powerful insights that naturally lead to an even smaller number of unique solutions, all applicable across the broadest possible set of customers. In other words, you need scale. Commercial Teaching is definitely *not* something you just want to leave in the hands of individual reps.

Commercial Teaching also requires you to think very differently about customer segmentation. While traditional segmentation schemes like geography, product silo, or industry vertical may be sufficient for sales rep deployment, the companies that do best at this approach have learned to also segment customers by need or behavior. If you can find a group of customers with similar needs—irrespective of where they are or what they sell—those customers will likely all react in a similar fashion to a common set of insights. For example, we have seen Commercial Teaching work very effectively around a common need to free up cash, or reduce employee churn, or improve workplace safety. In each of these cases, the suppliers in question helped customers think about that need in new and surprising ways by reframing their thinking, convincingly laying out the fully loaded costs of inaction, and then providing a credible course of action that naturally led back to the supplier's unique solution. And each did it across large groups of customers who under any traditional segmentation strategy would have appeared, superficially at least, to have nothing in common. The common denominator for insight, in other words, isn't geography, or size, or industry. It's a common set of needs.

We've done a great deal of work in our Marketing & Communications practice across the last three years helping members develop and implement various needs-based segmentation techniques, based on a number of best practices developed at some of the world's leading B2B companies. The one thing every company that's gone down this path has discovered is this: Needs analysis is not something you can afford to leave in the hands of your individual reps. If your reps' primary goal going into a sales call is to "discover" the customer's needs, you've lost the battle before you've even begun to fight, because, frankly, your customers don't want to have that conversation.

Alternatively, Commercial Teaching equips reps to teach customers what they really need by challenging the way they think about their business altogether, providing them with new means to address their toughest problems in ways they would have never identified on their own. Granted, there are some important conditions that must be met in order for this approach to work. Commercial Teaching must lead to your unique strengths, challenge customers' assumptions, catalyze action, and scale across customers. But when these conditions are met, it works—phenomenally well, in fact. And the reason why, as we saw, is because more than anything else customers are looking to suppliers to challenge their thinking and teach them something they don't know.

That said, once you've laid the groundwork for effective Commercial Teaching, your reps still have to go out and actually *talk* to customers. If they don't have the skills to challenge, even the most powerful insights will fall on deaf ears. So what does a "teaching conversation" actually sound like? Is it really all that different? Absolutely. It's not just that Challengers teach that sets them apart, it's the *way* that they teach that really matters most. World-class teaching conversations, it turns out, follow a very specific choreography, one that takes a traditional sales conversation and completely stands it on its head. Let's look at that next.

5

TEACHING FOR DIFFERENTIATION (PART 2):

HOW TO BUILD INSIGHT-LED CONVERSATIONS

ONCE YOU'VE AGREED on the unique benefits that clearly set you apart from the competition and you've identified a set of compelling insights that teach customers a new way to compete more effectively, how do you put it all together? Well, if you were to map a world-class teaching conversation—or teaching "pitch"—you'd find it moves through six discrete steps, each building directly to the next.

But before we get to the steps themselves, it's important to note the very strong emotional component of a well-designed teaching pitch. Frankly, this isn't so much about delivering a formal presentation as it's about telling a compelling story. Along the way, there should be some real drama, perhaps a bit of suspense, and maybe even a surprise or two. Ultimately, the goal is to take customers on a roller-coaster ride, leading first to a rather dark place before showing them the light at the end of the tunnel. And that light, of course, is your solution.

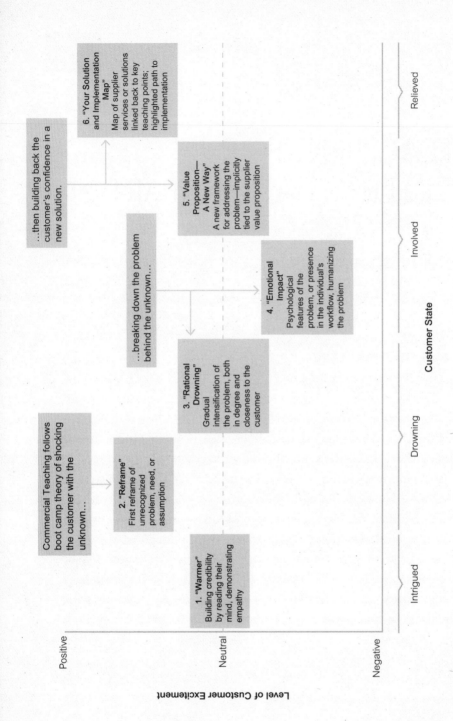

Figure 5.1. Deconstruction of a Commercial Teaching Pitch

Commercial Teaching follows boot camp theory of shocking the customer with the unknown…

…breaking down the problem behind the unknown…

…then building back the customer's confidence in a new solution.

1. "Warmer"
Building credibility by reading their mind, demonstrating empathy

2. "Reframe"
First reframe of unrecognized problem, need, or assumption

3. "Rational Drowning"
Gradual intensification of the problem, both in degree and closeness to the customer

4. "Emotional Impact"
Psychological features of the problem, or presence in the individual's workflow, humanizing the problem

5. "Value Proposition— A New Way"
A new framework for addressing the problem—implicitly tied to the supplier value proposition

6. "Your Solution and Implementation Map"
Map of supplier services or solutions linked back to key teaching points; highlighted path to implementation

Level of Customer Excitement

Positive

Neutral

Negative

Intrigued   Drowning   Involved   Relieved

Customer State

Source: CEB, CEB Sales Leadership Council, 2011.

A PURPOSEFUL CHOREOGRAPHY

If you're going to successfully convince reluctant customers to not only think differently, but act differently—in what is almost definitionally going to be a disruptive manner—then it's not enough for your teaching pitch to simply convey a "compelling business case" with data, charts, and graphs. No one ever sold anything off a spreadsheet alone. Done well, a teaching pitch makes customers feel sort of sick about all the money they're wasting, or revenue they're missing, or risk they're unknowingly exposed to. But if your story fails to engage both sides of the brain simultaneously—the rational and the emotional—it's too easy for your customer to make no decision even over a good decision, as logic alone is rarely enough to overcome the status quo. Disruptive change is as much about following your gut as it is about following your head.

So with that in mind, let's review the six steps of a world-class teaching pitch.

Step 1: The Warmer

After initial formalities (e.g., introductions, time check, agenda setting), a well-designed teaching pitch starts off with your assessment of your customer's key challenges. Rather than asking, "What's keeping you up at night?" you lay out what you're seeing and hearing as key challenges at similar companies. If you have it, this is a great place to provide benchmarking data. At the very least, this is where you share anecdotes from other companies that capture the challenges most likely of highest concern to your customer in ways that corroborate their own experience. (Never underestimate the value in being able to demonstrate to your customers that they're not alone when it comes to their most pressing challenges.) You then conclude your review by asking for their reactions. When you put it all together, it should sound something like, "We've worked with a number of companies similar to yours, and we've found that these three challenges come up again and again as by far the most troubling. Is that what you're seeing too, or would you add something else to the list?"

The whole point of step 1, of course, is to build credibility. Essentially, what you're saying to your customer is, "I understand your world," and "I'm not here to waste your time asking you to teach me about your business." It's an approach we've dubbed "Hypothesis-Based Selling." Rather than leading with open-ended *questions* about customers' needs, you lead with *hypotheses* of customers' needs, informed by your own experience and research. Ultimately, customers suffering from "solutions fatigue" love it not only because it makes the entire sale both faster and easier for them, but because it feels much more like a "get" than a "give"—they get your informed perspective rather than having to educate you with information you should have been able to figure out on your own. A Commercial Teaching pitch cuts right to the chase. It feels efficient. It honors the customer's time and shows that you've done your homework. In other words, you've just established yourself as someone worth talking to. Or, at the very least, for the especially resistant customers out there, you've just bought yourself another five minutes.

So what next? What are you going to do with the goodwill you've just established? Present your solution? Lay out your "value proposition"? That's the *last* thing you want to do now! Although it is the next step they're probably expecting, and it's absolutely the next thing a core-performing rep would do—and without a doubt what your competitor's sales rep did when he was sitting in the same customer's office an hour earlier.

Think about it. You just got your customer to warm up to you by talking about their business. Why in the world would you want to ruin all that goodwill by spouting off about *your* business? You haven't yet given them a reason to care. Instead, now you go to a place your customer never saw coming: the Reframe.

Step 2: The Reframe

This is *the* central moment of a Commercial Teaching pitch, as the entire conversation pivots off what you're about to do next.

Building off the challenges your customer just acknowledged in step 1, you now introduce a new perspective that connects those challenges to either a bigger problem or a bigger opportunity than they ever realized they had. Mind you, you're not expected to actually come up with the insight in the moment. For reasons we addressed in the previous section, that kind of spontaneous flash of brilliance is not only too hard, it's actually a bad idea. Rather, this is something you've come well prepared to discuss. (In fact, it may have been a brief mention of this insight that won you the visit in the first place.) That said, at this point, your goal isn't to lay out the explanations and implications of the insight in any great detail—that will come in a few minutes. Rather, the Reframe is simply about the insight itself. It's just the headline. And like any good headline, your goal is to catch your customer off guard with an unexpected viewpoint—to surprise them, make them curious, and get them wanting to hear more.

Remember, the reaction you're looking for here is definitely not, "Yes! I totally agree! That's exactly what we're working on!" but rather, "Huh, I never thought of it that way before." If your customer's first reaction to your insight is enthusiastic agreement, then you haven't actually taught them anything. And that's a dangerous place to be. Sure, it always feels great when your customer says, "I agree!" But if you've just articulated a problem they've already thought of, chances are pretty good they've already thought of a solution too. At best, you're now "teaching at the margins." Doing this is actually bad for *two* reasons. First, if you fail to provide unique insight, then you fail to provide unique value. Second, if your customers have already begun to consider possible solutions, you've lost a significant opportunity to skew their thinking toward your solution. Practically speaking, it's like failing to get ahead of the RFP. You're *responding* to customers' needs rather than *defining* them. And that's a recipe for increased commoditization.

If you're going to reframe, then be sure you really reframe. This is not the place to be timid, as the entire approach rests on your ability to surprise your customer and make them curious for more information. You've just bought yourself another five minutes. So what's next? Well, you've shown your customer a different way to think about their business, now you've got to show them why it matters.

Step 3: Rational Drowning

Rational Drowning is where you lay out the business case for why the Reframe in step 2 is worth your customer's time and attention.

So now it's time for the data, graphs, tables, and charts you need to quantify for the customer the true, often hidden, cost of the problem or size of the opportunity they'd completely overlooked. Rational Drowning is the numbers-driven rationale for why your customer should think differently about their business, but presented specifically in a way designed to make them squirm a little bit—to feel like they're drowning. Marketers often refer to this as the "FUD factor"—fear, uncertainty, and doubt. If your presentation is done well, the customer reaction in step 3 should be something like, "Wow, I had no idea we were wasting that kind of money!" or "I'd never thought of this as an opportunity before. We've got to get after this or we're going to really miss out!"

If you're going to put an ROI calculator in front of your customer, this is where it goes. But just remember the ROI that you're calculating. In a world-class teaching pitch a good ROI calculator calculates the ROI on solving the challenge you've just taught your customer they have, not the ROI on buying your solution. If your ROI calculator is explicitly about your products and services—as it almost inevitably is—then you're talking about the wrong thing. Before you demonstrate how your solution can economically solve a key customer challenge, you've got to convince the customer that that challenge is worth solving in the first place.

Putting steps 2 and 3 together, you've got to show them something new, and then show them why it matters. This is what good teaching is all about. *Great* teaching, however, requires something else: emotional impact.

Step 4: Emotional Impact

Emotional Impact is all about making absolutely sure that the customer sees themselves in the story you're telling. There's nothing more frustrating than laying out a compelling argument and hearing your customer say, "Yeah, I see what you're saying, and I'm sure it makes a lot of sense for a lot of your customers. But I'm struggling to see how this applies to us. We're different." Ugh. This is the sales version of that awkward moment when your date looks at you and says, "It's not you. It's me." Clearly, what they're trying to say is, "I have absolutely zero interest in anything you have to offer."

So what do you do now? How do you counter the "we're different" defense? For the core-performing rep, the response is predictable. If one chart wasn't enough, try two. If the PowerPoint deck didn't get you there, send the white paper. It's more of the same. But simply repeating the business case in greater detail will never get you past the "we're different" response. That's because you're solving for the wrong problem. The problem isn't that you've failed to make a logical presentation, the problem is you've failed to make an emotional connection. It's not that they don't believe your story, it's just that they don't see it as *their* story. You need to get them to internalize what you're telling them.

So how do you do that? Now you've got to make it personal. And this is where a Challenger rep's storytelling ability really comes into play. As the name implies, Emotional Impact isn't about the numbers; it's about the narrative. You've got to paint a picture of how other companies just like the customer's went down a similarly painful path by engaging in behavior that the customer will immediately recognize as typical of their own company.

The story, therefore, starts out with something like, "I understand you're a little bit different, but let me give you a sense of how we've seen this play out at similar companies . . ." And for this to work, whatever you say next has to *feel* immediately familiar (which is another reason why a deep understanding of the customer must be acquired *prior* to the sales call, not just during it). The reactions you're looking for are a rueful shake of the head, a wry smile, a thoughtful faraway look. Why? Because you're looking for the customer to replay the same scenario in their head as it *actually happened to them in their own company* just last week. Ideally, the customer's response to your story is something like, "Wow, it's like you work here or something. Yeah, we do that *all* the time. It just kills us." And that is how you slay the dragon of "we're just different": by creating an emotional connection between the pain in the story you're telling and the pain your customer feels every day inside their own organization. If your customer still thinks they're different after step 4, you either have the wrong customer or the wrong story.

But if you are successful, now you've got your customer bought in to the Reframe. They see the challenge or opportunity as their own, and now they're looking for a solution.

Step 5: A New Way

Coming into step 5 you've convinced the customer of the problem. Now you've got to convince them of the solution. This is a point-by-point review of the specific capabilities they would need to have in order to make good on whatever opportunity to make money, save money, or mitigate risk that you've just convinced them they're facing. As tempting as it might be at this point to launch into a review of how you can help, step 5 is still about the *solution*, not about the *supplier*. Facing a customer who enthusiastically agrees that they've got the very challenge your solution directly addresses, it is deeply tempting to talk specifically about how you can help. For most reps it simply feels like the obvious thing to do. But step 5 isn't a story about how much better customers' lives would be if they bought your stuff (which is what most reps want to talk about), it's about showing customers how much better their life would be if they just acted differently. It's about behaving differently, not buying differently.

Don't rush this. Before they buy *your* solution, the customer has to buy *the* solution. You're looking for your customer to say something like, "You're right, that makes total sense. That's what we need to do," or "That's the kind of company I want us to be." *Now* they're ready for step 6, Your Solution.

Step 6: Your Solution

If step 5 is about getting customers bought in to acting differently, the goal of step 6 is to demonstrate how your solution is better able than anyone else's to equip them to act differently. In many ways, of all six steps, this one is the most straightforward, as it's what reps have been trained to do from the very beginning. This is where you lay out the specific ways you can deliver the solution they've just agreed to in step 5 better than anyone else. It's also where all of the hard work around identifying your unique capabilities pays off, because they are front and center in step 6. After all, it would be absolutely crushing to get your customer all the way to step 6 and then have that deal go out to an RFP that you couldn't easily win. If your competition is still in the running at this point, then you have either failed to identify capabilities that are truly unique or you have failed to lead to them as convincingly as you'd hoped.

If, however, you've got this right, in steps 1–6 you've addressed both aspects of Commercial Teaching—the "commercial" and the "teaching"—in one conversation. You've taught the customer something new and valuable about their business (which is what they were looking for from the conversation), in a way that specifically leads them to value your capabilities over those of the competition (which is what you were looking for from the conversation).

Now, when you look back at all six steps together, ask yourself the following question: Where does the *supplier* first enter the conversation? Notice it's not until the very end in step 6. And for many reps, this is completely counterintuitive. After all, if I'm going to sell my solution to a customer, then the first thing I need to talk about is *my solution*—what it does, how it's different, how it helps. Right? Wrong! That's not the first thing you need to talk about, but the *last*, for a very simple reason: Your customer doesn't care.

That fact that your newly designed XZ-690 runs 15 percent faster, quieter, cooler, and cheaper than the competition just isn't that interesting to most customers. If it *is*, then why bother with a sales call at all? Just send them a quote and take the order over the phone. Better yet, sell it through an e-store on the Internet and get rid of your sales force altogether.

If, on the other hand, you're going to take sixty minutes of your customer's precious time for a face-to-face meeting, you'd better make sure that whatever you do with that time is valuable to your customer. Listening to a review of how your XZ-690 is going to save them time and money isn't. Talking about the customer's business in ways that help them boost productivity is.

Remember, in the Commercial Teaching world everything is built back from the finding that, in your customers' eyes, your primary value as a supplier is your ability to *teach* them something, not to *sell* them something. In the teaching world, the pitch isn't about the supplier at all. It's about the customer. As a result, the best sales reps have found that you can't win customers' interest and loyalty if you lead with your differentiators—all your products, services, and solutions—no matter how good they are. Instead, the best sales conversations present the customer with a compelling story about their business *first*, teach them something new, and then lead *to* their differentiators.

By placing your unique strengths in context at the end of a highly credible teaching pitch you completely change the customer's disposition toward your offering. But to get there, there has to be a flow to the conversation, a purposeful choreography where your solution is the natural outgrowth of your teaching, rather than the subject of your teaching. And that's a huge difference. Don't lead *with*, lead *to*. Remember, the real value of the interaction isn't what you sell; it's the insight you provide as part of the sales interaction itself.

A LOOK IN THE MIRROR

This teaching choreography allows you to very concretely audit and improve the sales conversations you're having with customers right now. How closely does *your* pitch follow this path? Does it lead with, or lead to? Here's a short quiz to compare your current approach with what you see here. Think right now about whatever piece of collateral, or slide deck, or capability brochure you typically take into a customer meeting. Specifically, think about the first four or five pages. What are they about? Most of the time it's something like this:

- What you believe in as a company. (Top favorites include "a cleaner world," "serving our customers," "innovating for the future," "our 150 years of experience," "our team of experienced professionals dedicated to helping our customers achieve their goals.")
- A review of all of your capabilities. (After all, you took the time and money to build out a solutions capability, and you want to make sure your customers understand all of the great

ways you can help. There's nothing more frustrating than customers who don't fully appreciate all the great things you can do for them.)

- A list of your top partners and customers, preferably accompanied by as many of their full-color logos as possible. (Nothing conveys credibility better than a long list of well-known customers who have placed their trust in you, right?)
- A map of all of your locations all over the world. (If your customers are going global, you want them to know you're right there with them, wherever that might be.)

Sound familiar? Are the first four pages of your sales materials all about you, or about the customer? Almost inevitably, it's the former. Not only do most reps lead with, rather than lead to, but almost all of the sales tools at their disposal do the same thing. It's a trend as predictable for organizations as it is for individuals.

So if you're going to build Challenger reps and ask them to teach your customers, for many companies one of the first steps will inevitably have to be a pretty significant review of the materials you provide them with to do that.

DEVELOPING A PURPOSEFUL CHOREOGRAPHY

So how do you *build* a Commercial Teaching message? The place to begin is actually at the end with step 6, your solution. You can't build a compelling story unless you first know what it's building to. You've got to have both clarity and agreement across your organization around the unique benefits that only you can offer your customers. That said, as you nail those benefits down, you'll want to focus in particular on the ones your customers currently *under*appreciate. Now that might feel counterintuitive at first. Wouldn't you do the opposite? Focus on the unique benefits that your customers truly value? After all, that's Marketing 101, right? Exactly.

But if you want to *teach* customers something new and not just reinforce what they already know, you'll need to ensure that the "punch line" of that teaching contains an element of surprise as well—a new and unexpected way to think about how you can help. Alternatively, if your customers already place high value on your benefits over those of the competition, you likely don't need to teach them anything at all. Just take their order. But beware: By focusing solely on the *known* value of your offering, you forgo an opportunity to challenge customers' thinking, which they value even more than whatever you're selling. You win their business in the short run, but potentially lose it over time. By helping customers think differently about *their* company, you ultimately want them to think differently about *your* company.

Once you've established clarity around step 6—Your Solution—your next stop in building a powerful Commercial Teaching conversation is step 2—the Reframe. You need to identify the core insight, or ah-ha! moment, that will get your customer to say, "Wow, I never thought about it that way before."

To get there, start with the unique benefits you've identified for step 6 and then ask yourself, "Why don't my customers value those benefits *already*?" What is it about how they view their world that precludes them from appreciating those benefits as much as we think they either could or should? That's the view you need to change. And to change it, you'll need to provide them with an alternate view (the Reframe), and then convince them that that alternate view—were they to pursue it—could either save or make them more money than they realized (step 3). After that, it's simply a matter of fleshing out the rest of the story to create a logical and compelling path from step 2 to step 6.

Put it all together and you get: "What's currently costing our customers more money than they realize, that only we can help them fix?" The answer to that question is the heart and soul of your Commercial Teaching pitch.

BUILDING THE INSIGHT GENERATION MACHINE

When you step back and consider the scope of what we're proposing here, you can begin to see how this approach reaches deep back into the organization. Yes, you need Challenger reps to deliver the teaching, but the actual construction of the conversation—the unique bene-fits, the surprising customer insights, the tightly packaged teaching choreography—require input from the entire commercial organization.

Many companies choose to shield sales reps from the complexity of the six-step choreography altogether by simplifying the approach into three key elements: (1) Providing customers with game-changing insight, (2) specifying and personalizing the potential impact of that insight, and (3) introducing your capabilities as the best possible means of acting on that insight. It's the same journey, but it's simply easier to process for reps traditionally accustomed to "leading with" rather than "leading to."

It's possible you've begun wondering: "Identifying unique benefits . . . segmenting customers by need . . . generating compelling customer insight . . . developing teaching-based collateral . . . For a book about individual sales performance, it seems like we've wandered a long way away from the individual rep." But remember, this book is absolutely about individual sales reps and how they can perform significantly bet-ter, yet you wouldn't want to leave any of *these* things in the hands of your individual reps. These are organizational capabilities, not indi-vidual skills. A critical lesson of the Challenger approach is the signifi-cant need for organizational involvement to make it truly sustainable and not just the result of incidental sales rep excellence. Few but the very best of your reps could pull off this kind of teaching on their own con-sistently over time.

When sales leaders first see Commercial Teaching, they usually tell us something like, "I'm having a hard enough time getting my guys to *sell*, and now you want them to *teach*? Good luck!" But it doesn't have to be that way. At least in terms of teaching, the most important steps you can take to migrate your sales force closer to the Challenger profile have less to do with the individual reps themselves and much more to do with the organization that supports them. In fact, in many ways, Commercial Teaching is likely *easier* for individual reps than what we're asking them to do right now. Much of the heavy lifting necessary to its success happens long before an individual rep ever gets in front of a customer.

To understand why, think about the journey from transactional selling to solutions selling that just about every B2B sales organization has undertaken across the last five to fifteen years (see figure 1.1 on page 7). As part of that move, sales skill requirements have gone up dramatically. With transactional selling, reps sold largely on product features and benefits; in the new world of solution selling, reps probe for individual customer needs in the moment, allowing them to suggest specifically tailored solutions to whatever they hear in response. In its purest form, solution selling is customization in the moment. It's an incredibly high bar for any sales rep. It's no wonder, really, that sales organizations all over the world struggle mightily to help their teams make this transition.

With Commercial Teaching, you can significantly back off on your expectations for individual customization ability, as the organization steps in to offer crucial support around the very thing that customers have told us they value most in supplier interactions, namely the sharing of commercial insight. The reps' primary job shifts from discovering needs to guiding a conversation. That allows the organization to lay out the framework for that conversation in advance—to "chalk the field," as one head of sales put it.

There are a number of ways in which that conversation might still take an unexpected turn or go off the rails altogether, and individual skill is still hugely important in allowing the best reps to navigate those scenarios better than anyone else, but Commercial Teaching places significant guardrails around the sales interaction to provide real support for the rep.

First, the customer's needs are *prescoped*. Reps don't start with a blank sheet of paper and diagnose each customer's needs individually. Much of that work has been done inside the organization through better segmentation and customer analysis, significantly reducing the burden on the one skill reps probably struggle with the most.

Second, the conversation is *prescripted*. A teaching rep still has to interact with the customer in a live setting, answering questions and adapting to unanticipated objections. However, the rep's opening set of hypotheses is already laid out in detail, and every step along the way is clearly marked through the teaching choreography. Because the teaching pitch follows the same talking points again and again, reps will naturally improve as they learn from experience, becoming more compelling over time. In that respect, Commercial Teaching supported by the organization is much more concrete than running an open-ended needs analysis. It's easier for reps to learn, and easier for managers to coach.

Finally, the solution the rep is working toward is *predefined*. The burden on the rep to determine the right solution for an individual customer is significantly reduced, as the solution is largely determined in advance through organizational identification of the supplier's unique benefits and needs-based segmentation of customers. One company we work with refers to these prebuilt solutions as "Happy Meals," based on McDonald's famous "meal solution" for young children. They're off-the-shelf solutions that feel customized to customers, because they're well tailored in advance to those customers' most common needs.

Of course, this approach still requires greater skill than the simple world of transactional selling. But compare it with a world of classic solution selling or "consultative selling" where reps are expected to figure all of this out on their own. While your stars will get it right at least some of the time, your core reps will struggle mightily all of the time. But if you've done your homework inside the organization to build a solid teaching interaction to begin with, your reps are far better prepared to succeed when they're in front of the customer.

So who should do the work? Commercial Teaching is as much a team sport as an individual one. Just as you'll need to align individual reps to the Challenger profile to make it work, you'll need to align sales and marketing around the core capabilities implicit in the Commercial Teaching choreography:

1. Identify your unique benefits.
2. Develop commercial insight that challenges customers' thinking.
3. Package commercial insight in compelling messages that "lead to."
4. Equip reps to challenge customers.

Commercial Teaching also provides a concrete and very actionable road map for addressing arguably one of the toughest challenges in all of B2B sales and marketing, namely getting the two functions to work together in the first place.

Given the chance, any head of sales or marketing will be happy to regale you with examples of the historically poor—or nonexistent—collaboration between the two functions. At best in most organizations there's a thinly veiled antipathy across the sales/marketing divide. At worst, it's outright hostility. We've all seen the statistics. Eighty percent of marketing collateral winds up in the trash, while 30 percent of sales time is spent reproducing the very collateral they just threw away.

The underlying cause of much of this discord typically goes unaddressed. Most companies fail to define an agreed-upon framework for what the two functions should actually do together in the first place. Many commercial executives who lament the need for greater sales and marketing "integration" fail to consider the problem from the opposite perspective, which is: What *shouldn't* they do together?

Commercial Teaching provides a road map for integrating around a limited number of activities that truly matter. The approach defines a very specific framework for "what good looks like" for the entire commercial organization, allowing for the identification of concrete roles, tasks, goals, and responsibilities. For example, only marketing has the tools, the expertise, and the time to generate the insights necessary to challenge customers both scalably and repeatedly. As the head of marketing at a large telecommunications company put it, marketing must serve as the "insight generation machine" that keeps reps well equipped with quality teaching material that customers will find compelling. Sales, on the other hand, will have to ensure that reps have the knowledge, skills, and coaching necessary to go out and use that insight in a convincing manner to actually challenge customers. It's a symbiotic relationship around a core principle.

Either way, at the end of the day your message library, your collateral, and your pitch can't be static. They must constantly evolve to stay current with the customer's business environment and with a competitive, dynamic landscape. This is a big job—hundreds of products, dozens of customer segments, multiple channels, and a customer environment that evolves on a quarterly basis. Therefore, Commercial Teaching isn't a one-time exercise, it's an "always-on" capability. With input from the sales force—and at their behest—organizations must invest in training marketers to articulate differentiators and constantly source fresh and compelling teaching messages.

MAKE SURE YOUR TEACHING PITCH IS "BOLD"

We see a lot of companies slip into "safe mode" as they develop their teaching pitches. They might start with something insightful and genuinely provocative, but as more and more people get their hands on it internally, it gets watered down to the point where it's more of a suggestion than a provocation.

A great tool we've seen to ensure that teaching pitches don't lose their edge as they work their way through the organization is the "SAFE-BOLD Framework," developed by Neil Rackham and KPMG. The framework functions as a grading exercise for evaluating the strength of a teaching pitch. To quote Neil and KPMG, "A successful teaching pitch must do four things well. First, it must be *big*. Done well, it will be seen by the customer as more expansive and farther-reaching than an ordinary idea. Second, it must be *innovative*. It has to push the envelope with new, often untested and unique approaches. Third, it must be *risky*. Big ideas mean that we are asking our own companies and our customers to take a big risk in adopting our idea. And lastly, it must be *difficult*. The idea itself must be hard to do—either because of scale, uncertainty, or politics—otherwise, why would a customer hire you to fix it for them?"

The framework is a simple tool that forces you to grade a potential teaching pitch along these four dimensions. The best ideas will score closer to the "BOLD" end of the continuum—they will be big, they will outperform (from a riskiness perspective), they will be leading-edge (in terms of innovation), and they will be difficult to implement for the customer. At the other end of the spectrum are the "SAFE" ideas, which, in contrast, are small, feel easily achievable (in terms of risk), are "follower" ideas (versus progressive, innovative ideas), and are seen as easy to implement.

The way Neil and the KPMG team employed this tool was to ask a group of KPMG client advisers to brainstorm a Challenger pitch to a client and then present that pitch to an audience of internal peers, who in turn graded the pitch using the SAFE-BOLD framework. KPMG tells us that this has now become a part of

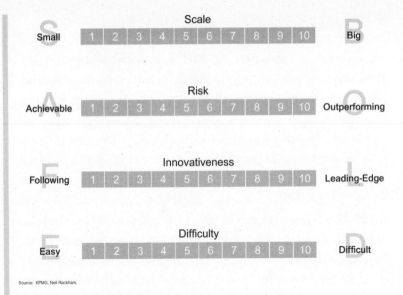

		Scale											
Small	1	2	3	4	5	6	7	8	9	10	Big

		Risk											
Achievable	1	2	3	4	5	6	7	8	9	10	Outperforming

		Innovativeness											
Following	1	2	3	4	5	6	7	8	9	10	Leading-Edge

		Difficulty											
Easy	1	2	3	4	5	6	7	8	9	10	Difficult

Source: KPMG, Neil Rackham.

Figure 5.2. The SAFE-BOLD Framework

the internal vernacular for the organization, with client advisers cautioning peers against watering down and "making too SAFE" their customer pitches.

Remember, Relationship Builders are everywhere, not just in sales, and chances are pretty good that somewhere along the line, a senior-level Relationship Builder—maybe somebody in marketing or corporate communications, maybe a senior line executive—will temper the message of the pitch, fearful that it will come across as confrontational or unsettling to the customer.

One of the classic Relationship Builder modifications to a great teaching pitch is to pull the "who we are and what we do" slides from the *back* of the pitch deck (where they belong in a proper teaching pitch) and put them in the front of the deck. Relationship Builders feel the need to establish credibility up front by throwing around company size and factoids and engaging in some high-profile customer name-dropping. They are uncomfortable leading with insight and letting their insights establish credibility for them.

As soon as you're not looking, Relationship Builders will take out their belt sanders and smooth out the edges of your sharp pitch. They'll soften it until you barely recognize it, pushing it to the SAFE end of the continuum.

But being a little unsettling is the point of a Challenger approach: to be provocative, to challenge, and therefore to be seen as differentiated by the customer. Without an edge, you sound just like everybody else. Remember, while Relationship Builders seek to reduce or defuse tension, Challengers constructively use tension to their advantage.

So what does Commercial Teaching look like and feel like in reality? Now that we've laid out the theory of the approach, we can see it in action at two real companies: W. W. Grainger, Inc., and ADP Dealer Services.

COMMERCIAL TEACHING CASE STUDY #1: W. W. GRAINGER, INC., AND THE POWER OF PLANNING THE UNPLANNED

W. W. Grainger, Inc., based in Lake Forest, Illinois, is a $7 billion distributor of maintenance, repair, and operations (MRO) equipment and supplies, serving nearly two million companies primarily across the United States and Canada. Grainger provides one-stop shopping for the wide range of equipment companies need to keep their facilities, plants, and offices running safely, smoothly, and efficiently. All told, the company stocks several hundred thousand different products—from tools, pumps, and safety supplies to electrical equipment and janitorial supplies—which they deliver through branches, a heavily trafficked e-store, and of course the famous Grainger product catalog. Much of its sales volume is driven by both inside and field-based sales reps working with customers to establish long-term customer purchase agreements.

As powerful as Grainger's broad product portfolio can be in serving customers' many and diverse needs, the company's impressive scope can be overwhelming. Faced with such a daunting array of choices, over the years, some customers have slipped into buying individual products reactively, based simply on past purchase patterns and opportunistic need, rather than taking the time to sit down with Grainger and consider how to manage their overall MRO spend more wisely, despite the fact that many companies' total MRO spend can easily reach into the tens of millions of dollars. In the view of many customers, it's just a bunch of hammers, gloves, light bulbs, pumps, and generators. "We've got more important things to do," the thinking goes, "than spend our time worrying about *that* stuff." The result for Grainger? Over time, many customers had come to think of Grainger merely as a transactional supplier rather than a strategic partner. Need a hammer? Go to Grainger. Need a pump? Go to Grainger. Need business advice on competing more effectively? Not so much. It simply never occurred to many customers that Grainger might be able to help with anything beyond great products at great prices. So when it came time for those customers to renew their contracts, that's what they wanted to talk about: price.

Now, you could argue that there are certainly worse problems to have than customers who think about you primarily as the company with great products at great prices. But if your primary goal as a business is to drive deeper customer relationships through broader, more strategic "solutions," it's actually a pretty tough place to be. It's hard to drive organic growth and deepen customer relationships when your customers think of you by and large as a transactional supplier of relatively unimportant products. In the end, you become relegated to the customer's facilities management team, or worse, procurement, where you wind up haggling over short-term pricing rather than long-term value creation.

So Grainger had a problem. As Debra Oler, Grainger's vice president and general manager of Grainger Brand, put it, if the company was going to establish itself as a true solutions provider in the minds of its customers, it had to change the way those customers thought about the company. They needed to build a convincing story, not about how Grainger can sell you more hammers, but about how it can help you improve your bottom line by saving you money.

To do that, Grainger first had to solve an even bigger challenge. The real problem wasn't so much that customers failed to think about Grainger strategically, but that they failed to think of their own MRO spend strategically. It's hard to be perceived as an important partner when your customers think of you as only touching an unimportant part of the business.

So long before Grainger could change customers' minds about how they thought about it, they first had to change customers' minds about how they thought about *themselves*. They had to show them that the millions of dollars they spend every year in MRO purchases is not only a sizable investment, but more important, one that, if managed properly, could save them millions of dollars. Indeed, in tracking customers' purchase habits for several years, Grainger had discovered that most companies were purchasing MRO products extremely inefficiently, and those habits were costing them millions of dollars that they had no idea they could be saving. In other words, Grainger had discovered an opportunity to teach customers something new about their business—a way to rethink MRO spend—that could free up huge amounts of cash they could then use on much more important things than hammers. In terms of insight, they had a slam dunk.

In terms of Commercial Teaching, however, Grainger needed the other crucial piece of the story. Before teaching customers how to save millions of dollars by thinking differently about their MRO spend, Grainger had to make sure that this insight naturally led customers to prefer Grainger over the wide range of alternative MRO suppliers. To do that, Deb and the team first had to answer the single question, "Why should our customers buy from us over anyone else?" As it turned out, that question wasn't nearly as easy to answer as they'd anticipated. As Deb tells it, one colleague suggested, for example, that they tout their massive product line as truly differentiating. Whereupon Deb asked, "Do none of our competitors offer a wide range of products?"

"No," the answer came back, "there are a few guys out there that have a pretty wide range of products as well—at least for some of the categories we serve."

"That won't work, then. What else is there?" asked Deb.

"Well, we've got stores all over the country. Wherever you are, you can find a Grainger branch."

"So customers can't meet their MRO needs through other retail outlets?" Deb asked.

"No, there are other companies out there with stores . . ."

"That's not it either, then. What else?"

And around they went, looking for the set of capabilities that truly set Grainger apart. And frankly, it proved to be much harder than most on the team would have thought. As Deb put it, "For a while, it really took us to a dark place. After all, what *were* we better at than anyone else? Were we really any different?"

It's a difficult question for most companies. When you sit down to really define the specific set of capabilities that sets you apart, once you cross off "innovative," "customer-focused," "solutions-oriented," "market leader," "great people," "trusted," and "rich history" from your list, many executives land in the same dark place Grainger did. And now you've got to roll up your sleeves and set about the hard work of identifying real capabilities that only you can offer. For Grainger, that kind of clarity came only after a large number of leader-led customer interviews, a great deal of market research, some robust data analysis of customer spending tendencies, and a number of cross-functional brainstorming sessions designed to capture as complete a picture of market perceptions as possible.

In the end, all of that work led Grainger to two important conclusions. First, most companies were spending far too much on purchasing MRO products every year, because they failed to appreciate how certain buying behaviors were costing them huge amounts of money. Second, while other suppliers might carry a wide range of products or maintain a convenient network of retail outlets, only Grainger did it all, and on a scale that allowed customers partnered with Grainger to eliminate those costs by avoiding unnecessary or "cautionary" MRO purchases. Whatever you needed, wherever you needed it, whenever you needed it, Grainger could provide it, so you didn't have to buy it "just in case." In other words, Grainger's distinctive *combination* of capabilities put the company in a unique position to help customers free up surprising amounts of operating expense, and provided a powerful opportunity to shift customers' view of Grainger from transactional supplier to strategic partner.

Grainger then took those insights and built them into a conversation titled "The Power of Planning the Unplanned," a world-class example of a Commercial Teaching conversation. This is the kind of content organizations need to provide the frontline sales force in order to make Commercial Teaching work beyond the star-performing Challenger reps. In fact, Grainger reps bring the "Power of Planning the Unplanned" deck into almost every sales call because it absolutely hits the heart of the company's differentiated value proposition. For Grainger, the goal of this conversation is to change the way that customers think about the company. But to get them there, the Grainger rep first needs to get customers to change the way they think about their own MRO spend. That's how the conversation is set up from the very beginning—as a conversation about the customer's MRO spend, not about Grainger's capabilities.

So as you might imagine, the Grainger sales rep requests the meeting in the first place in order to share some important insights Grainger has learned about how most companies could save a lot of money simply by thinking differently about how they manage their MRO spend. In fact, take a look at the agenda for the sales call:

What We Want To Share With You

- Industry studies of MRO purchases

- Business challenges of unplanned purchases that impact your bottom line:
  - Inventory
  - Productivity
  - Service gaps

- Grainger's solution to those challenges

© 2008 W.W. Grainger Inc.   *GRAINGER*

From the very start of the conversation, everything is squarely focused on the customer. Remember, customers want to talk about *their* business, not *your* solution, and that's exactly how Grainger positions the meeting. First and foremost, the agenda is laid out as a "get" for the customer, not a "give." It's Grainger saying, "We're here to help you think smarter about a part of your business where we have deep expertise." That's the positioning; now we're ready to go. First stop, step 1, the Warmer:

You Face Many Challenges Daily

Availability · Facility Security · Delivery Times · JIT Inventory

Training · Lost Work Days · Inventory Level · Freight · Power Outages

Workers Compensation · Hard to Find Item · Budget Cuts · Productivity Improvements · Air Quality

Safety · Cash Flow · Supplier out of Stock · Ordering · HazMat

Employee Satisfaction · Repair Parts · OSHA Audits · Technical Support

Different Brands · Production Line Issues · Cross Referencing · Testing & Audits · Product Quality

© 2008 W.W. Grainger Inc.

GRAINGER

The Warmer starts with the customer's challenges. So the opening is, "We know you face a host of challenges every day, such as production line issues, workers' comp costs, maintenance and safety issues. Especially those challenges that are critical to keeping your business open and running every single day." After reviewing a couple issues and providing some general color from other companies, the rep then asks the customer to select for discussion one or two that are particularly pressing in their organization.

The idea is to get the customer pulled into the conversation right away and talking about their challenges relative to what Grainger has already seen at other companies. Grainger has found that this one page can lead to an incredibly robust and valuable conversation—all because the rep led with a hypothesis of customer need rather than an open-ended question to "discover" customer need.

Done well, at this point the conversation feels less like a sales presentation and more like two colleagues commiserating about common challenges. It's a connection born of shared experience and a great way to start a conversation.

Yet while the Grainger rep may have built a connection at this point, he or she hasn't actually taught the customer anything new. That happens in step 2, the Reframe.

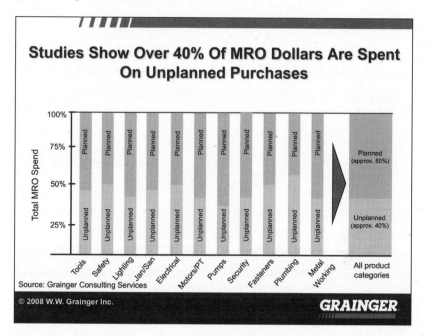

Studies Show Over 40% Of MRO Dollars Are Spent On Unplanned Purchases

Source: Grainger Consulting Services

© 2008 W.W. Grainger Inc.

GRAINGER

To change the way customers think about their MRO spend, Grainger starts by breaking that spend into its typical categories: tools, safety, lighting, janitorial, and so on. For many companies the total spend in any *one* of these categories can easily represent hundreds of thousands of dollars or more, depending on the company's size. This will all look very familiar to the customer.

However, what's *not* familiar to customers is a completely different way to think about this spend. Using a relatively straightforward graphic, the rep shifts the customer's perspective from vertical product categories to horizontal purchase tendencies: from *what* they buy to *how* they buy. They do that by introducing the idea of "planned" versus "unplanned" purchases.

The rep explains, "Planned purchases are products and parts that you buy very frequently, usually on a regular cycle and budgeted for in advance. *Un*planned purchases, on the other hand, are products and repair parts that you buy at the last minute, usually in response to some unforeseen need or problem." The distinction's important, because what companies don't realize is how the unplanned part of MRO spend—the seemingly one-off, innocuous purchases of an extra hammer here, or a replacement pump there—can add up to a huge amount in any given year and actually have strategic consequences for a company. Grainger has determined from its research that a full 40 percent of a typical company's MRO spend is for unplanned purchases. When you add that up across all categories of MRO spend combined, unplanned purchase spend is bigger than any one individual product category, representing millions of dollars in last minute, one-off spending.

Notice, the rep hasn't yet built the full business case for why the distinction matters—that's still coming—but at this point he or she has at least piqued the customer's interest. They're curious to hear more. After all, you've just told them that their second biggest category of MRO spend—unplanned purchases—is one they've never even thought to track before. Now they're wondering what that might mean for their business. Remember, the litmus test for the Reframe is simply to get your customer to say, "Huh, I'd never really thought about it that way before," and this shift in perspective from what they buy to how they buy is a great example of how to do that well.

Now the rep is ready to build a solid business case for why it matters. On to step 3, Rational Drowning.

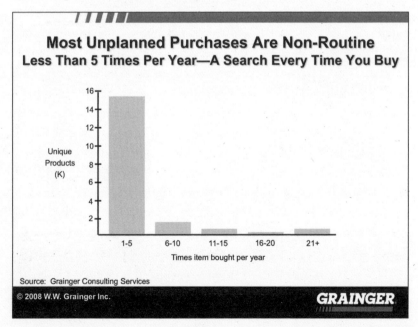

Most Unplanned Purchases Are Non-Routine
Less Than 5 Times Per Year—A Search Every Time You Buy

Source: Grainger Consulting Services

© 2008 W.W. Grainger Inc.

GRAINGER

Using data from its own analysis of several years' worth of customer spend data, Grainger uses the next several slides to build out the story of the often overlooked, but very real cost of unplanned purchases. "In fact," the Grainger rep continues, "it's probably worse than you think. A huge number of the purchases you make aren't just unplanned— they're infrequent. Most you make only once. Yet each one requires additional time, effort, people, and money to complete."

This is Grainger using their expertise to teach the customer something about their business. For the customer, it's valuable insight. For Grainger, it's an effective means to turn interest into action by building a rational business case that makes the customer feel real discomfort around a problem they'd never realized they had. If Grainger has a long-standing relationship with a particular customer, the rep will often review their purchase history with the company to ensure the story is as compelling as possible. It's hard to say you're different when you're looking at your very own data.

So what's the impact of all of these unplanned purchases? Well, it's pretty dramatic.

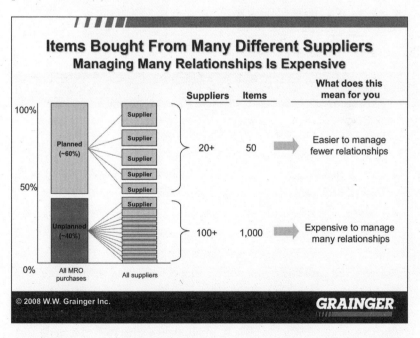

While most companies work with a small number of suppliers for planned purchases, they often have hundreds of suppliers for unplanned purchases, because every item is purchased from whichever supplier can get it to you right away. And the cost of spreading 40 percent of your MRO spend across that many different suppliers can be huge, as there's no leverage there. Every item is purchased at the last minute at full retail.

Even worse than the additional *direct* costs of unplanned purchases, however, are the unseen but dramatically high *indirect* costs.

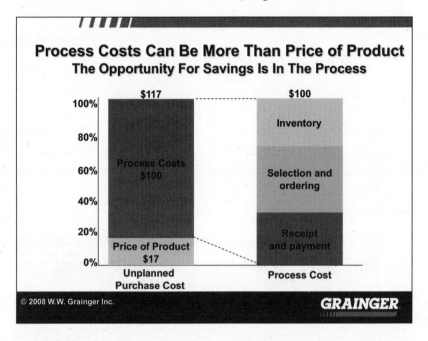

Process Costs Can Be More Than Price of Product
The Opportunity For Savings Is In The Process

$117 — 100% — $100

Process Costs $100

Price of Product $17

Inventory

Selection and ordering

Receipt and payment

Unplanned Purchase Cost

Process Cost

© 2008 W.W. Grainger Inc.

GRAINGER

The real cost of unplanned purchases comes from all of the necessary but typically overlooked process costs associated with buying something you hadn't planned for. You've got to take the time to find the part, generate an invoice, call the supplier, place the order, inventory whatever you bought, and then run paperwork and payment on the purchase. All told, any single unplanned purchase can involve five to ten different people across your company and incur huge amounts of unseen cost when you add up all the time, effort, paperwork, and people necessary to buy it. More often than not the very act of buying an unplanned item is vastly more expensive than the item itself.

At this point, the customer is likely beginning to feel a little sick about all these unplanned purchases. This is happening every day in their organization, and they've never really thought of it this way before.

They're thinking, "Great, that hammer I bought last week for $17 actually cost me $117! If I multiply that by 40 percent of my total MRO spend, how am I even staying in business?" It's meant to be a real gut punch—a rational argument designed to evoke an emotional reaction.

But just in case the customer is still skeptical of the problem at this point, Grainger turns the dial one more time. The conversation now moves to step 4, Emotional Impact. Now they make it personal.

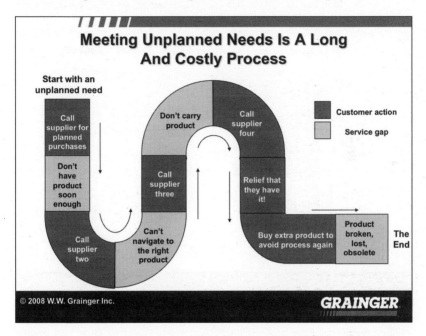

To ensure that the customer truly sees themselves in the story Grainger is telling, Grainger uses a slide they like to call the "Pain Chain" to illustrate how nearly every company acts when something important breaks down that they need to replace in a hurry.

Let's say that a hard-to-find coil on the twenty-year-old air-conditioning system in your CEO's office goes out in midsummer. Well, it's hot, and it's your CEO, so clearly you've got to get the thing fixed as soon as possible. So what do you do?

The first thing you likely do is call one of your go-to suppliers for planned purchases. Surely they can help. But after twenty minutes on hold, you learn that they've just sold out of the part and won't have any more for at least two weeks. So you try another supplier you've worked with once or twice in the past, but they don't carry the part at all. After twenty minutes on hold, a third supplier tells you that according to their inventory system they should have two in stock, but they can't find them on the shelf back in the warehouse. Now you're getting frustrated. Two hours on the phone—mostly listening to really bad adult contemporary music—and you've got nothing but bad news to report to your increasingly impatient—and sweaty—CEO.

Feeling a little desperate, you call the fourth and final supplier in the greater metropolitan area. They're all the way across town, but that ceased to matter about ninety minutes ago. Great! They've got the part! So you pull two guys off the production line, put the hastily generated paperwork in their hands, and send them across town in rush-hour traffic to pick up the part. An hour and a half later, when they get there, they call you up and say, "Hey, boss, they've actually got three of these things. You want that we should buy another one, just to be safe?" Well, you never want to go through *this* again, so you tell them, "Just buy all three and get back here as fast as you can!"

You use one part to repair the air conditioner, and you put the other two in the back corner of the warehouse on a shelf Grainger likes to call the "Parts Orphanage" where they just sit and gather dust. You probably won't need them next year. Or the year after that. And when you finally do, the whole system is likely obsolete and needs to be replaced anyway. But if you think about it, not only are those parts that you'll never use, but more important, that's valuable cash you've just tied up in inventory that you don't actually need, simply because you never want to have to go through the pain of having to buy that part again. And that's cash you could be using for far more important things that you actually *do* need.

Dramatic? Yes. But Grainger's story is completely believable and credible. That's because it's based on real customer behavior (this is where all those customer interviews really pay off). More important, however, it's dramatic for a reason. The story is intentionally designed to generate an emotional response from customers. They need to see themselves in the picture you're painting. They should feel the pain as if it were their story you were telling. As one customer put it when they saw the Pain Chain, "Wow, you know us too well! We play a starring role in that movie every single day!" And that's the point. To get the customer to "own" the story, ensure that they see unplanned purchases as a problem that absolutely applies to them.

Now the transition into step 5, where Grainger can paint the picture of a New Way.

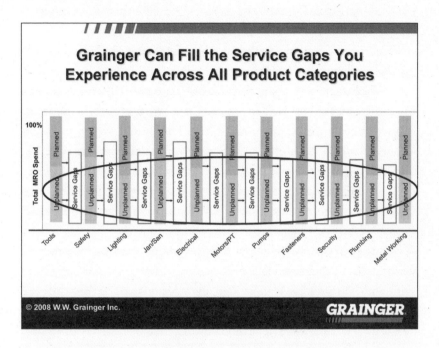

To get to the actual solution, Grainger transitions from the personal to the organizational: "Now, that's the problem with just one unplanned purchase in one category. The kicker is, you do that again and again across every category of MRO spend. So even if you were able to get your hands around unplanned purchases in one category, the larger problem is still there. And no company is structured to effectively manage this spend across every category.

"But imagine if you could. The problem represents a huge opportunity if you can get your hands around it. Unplanned purchases represent a huge amount of unnecessary spend and unnecessary inventory costs. It's money you could be spending on more important things. And that's a problem that Grainger—given its specific capability set—is uniquely positioned to solve for you."

At this point, the conversation turns to how Grainger can help. Finally, we're ready to start talking about Grainger's solution. If you're an existing customer, they've got your actual data and can start mapping out a plan. If they don't work with you much, they use this conversation to suggest a diagnostic of your unplanned purchases. Either way, all of the hard work that Deb and the team did earlier to map out Grainger's unique benefits is now laid out, specifically in terms of how they help customers solve the unplanned purchase challenge that Grainger has just taught them they have.

It's an absolutely fantastic example of Commercial Teaching because the heart and soul of the conversation is a set of insights designed to help customers operate more profitably. That said, did you see where Grainger and its capabilities first come up in the conversation? Not until the very end. There's no mention of Grainger's capabilities, stores, Web sites, history, size, product catalog, etc., *anywhere* across the first two-thirds of this conversation. That's because this isn't a story about Grainger; it's a story about the *customer* and how they can put money back into their operating budget that they didn't even realize they were wasting. From the customer's perspective, the fact that Grainger has a solution to the problem is more a happy coincidence. For them, the real value of the interaction is the quality of Grainger's insight.

Customers come away from this conversation thinking very differently not only about their MRO spend, but also about the role Grainger can play in significantly reducing that spend over time. Grainger is no longer the place to buy $17 hammers, but rather the partner to work with in order to avoid buying $117 hammers. By placing Grainger's unique strengths in context—at the end of a highly credible teaching pitch—the company completely changes customers' disposition toward their offering. But to get there, there has to be a flow to the pitch, a specific "choreography." And that's really the fundamental shift of Commercial Teaching. It's a move from leading *with* your unique strengths to one where carefully constructed teaching interactions very deliberately lead the customer *to* your unique strengths. Your solution isn't the subject of your teaching but the natural outgrowth of your teaching. Remember, from the customer's perspective, the real value of the interaction isn't what you sell, it's the quality of the insight you provide as part of the sales interaction itself.

COMMERCIAL TEACHING CASE STUDY #2: ADP DEALER SERVICES' PROFIT CLINIC SEMINARS

ADP Dealer Services, a division of Automatic Data Processing, is a leading provider of enterprise software to car, truck, and other kinds of vehicle dealerships around the world. When Kevin Hendrick, then the head of sales for ADP, first saw our work on Commercial Teaching in 2008, the company was facing a real problem. While the economy was still in relatively strong shape, the team at Dealer Services was already tracking a number of early warning signs in the automotive industry that didn't bode well for the near future. Not only had retail car sales declined steadily for the last three years, but more troubling, the U.S. car industry was facing a significant overpopulation of dealerships, the number of which, in response to shrinking demand, was now dramatically declining. Ultimately, across the three years from 2007 to 2010 the number of new and used auto dealerships in the U.S. decreased from 21,200 to 18,460. Now, if you're a provider of enterprise software solutions to auto dealerships, think for a minute about what those numbers mean. In the course of just a few short years, the company was facing a 15 percent decline of its total addressable market in a key market segment as potential customers simply vanished.

Tougher still, as part of a publicly traded company, ADP Dealer Services was naturally looking to post strong organic growth over that same period. But how in the world do you grow a company in a declining market? That's incredibly difficult. Really, you have only one choice: Aggressively increase market share while vigorously preventing customer defection. In this world, if you're going to win new business, you're going to have to take it away from someone else.

But that wasn't going to be easy. While dislodging an incumbent supplier is always a challenge, the company was simultaneously battling a rise in small competitors, each competing aggressively against only a specific piece of Dealer Services' broader capability set. As an industry-leading supplier, ADP offered a unique value proposition encompassing technology solutions for every aspect of an automotive dealership, including digital marketing, vehicle sales, service sales, and even parts solutions. Small competitors, on the other hand, focused on only one piece of that puzzle, such as software designed to run just the service center, or just the sales office. These vendors approached customers with a very different kind of message, emphasizing vast potential savings by buying "only the software you most urgently need." And as you might imagine, in a world of concerned customers looking to survive, that message was resonating strongly.

Put it all together and ADP Dealer Services was looking at a potentially painful year. On the one hand, they were losing margin to customers increasingly focused on cost containment as their industry imploded around them. On the other, they were losing sales to upstart competitors aggressively playing on those fears to drive customers into price-based, transactional sales of stripped-down, stand-alone products. Yet the true irony of the situation was the fact that the very heart and soul of Dealer Services' value proposition was their unique ability to help dealers reduce cost. And if there was ever a time when this message should resonate, one would think that this would have been it. But that didn't happen. Customers simply couldn't see past the total price tag. Dealer Services reps would go into a sales call leading with all of ADP's unique and powerful capabilities to save customers money, and the dealers would respond, "That's great, but I've got another guy that says he can do just the part I need right now for a *lot* less. I'd like to work with you guys, but only if you throw all this other stuff out and knock 30 percent off the price of what's left." Painful.

It's no wonder, then, that when Kevin saw the work on Commercial Teaching he had a bit of a "lightbulb moment." He realized that a large part of the problem was that ADP Dealer Services reps were "leading with," not "leading to." If Dealer Services was going to get customers to think differently about its broader solution, the company first had to get dealers to think differently about the costs associated with their software choices. Because ADP knew something about the implications of those choices that customers themselves didn't yet realize: In their efforts to save money, all of their investments in one-off software systems for individual parts of the business were causing them huge operational inefficiency and redundancy that was ultimately costing them money, not saving it.

With that insight in mind, Dealer Services set out to build a comprehensive Commercial Teaching capability, spanning two key initiatives.

The first was to build a better story. While the company had a clear understanding of the unique benefits that set their solution apart, they needed messaging leading *to* those benefits, rather than *with* them. So the company's sales operations and marketing teams designed a powerful story called "Total Dealer Spend," featuring a data-based analysis of the surprisingly costly but hidden impact of inefficient IT systems on overall dealership profitability. On average, they found, dealerships work with twelve different vendors, resulting in up to 40 percent redundant costs—costs ADP Dealer Services could eliminate through their single-supplier solution. Not surprisingly, like the Grainger story, the central goal of Dealer Services' approach was to evoke an emotional as well as a rational response. Dealers were surprised—and often deeply troubled—to learn that they were unnecessarily spending huge amounts of money at a time when they could least afford to do so.

ADP's second key initiative was to build a series of customer seminars—called Profit Clinics—designed to provide dealers with in-person insights into how to run their companies more profitably. The clinics are exactly what they sound like—free seminars offered by Dealer Services specifically designed to help customers assess the costs of inefficient and duplicative work created by overlapping IT systems. The focus is squarely on the insight.

Of course, as you might imagine, the seminars are also constructed to follow a Commercial Teaching choreography. The one thing ADP Dealer Services does *not* talk about for the first two-thirds of the seminar is ADP Dealer Services. It's not about the supplier, it's about the customer. Just like Grainger, after a Warmer, there's the Reframe (i.e., "The software decisions you're making in order to save money are actually costing you money"), then the Rational Drowning and Emotional Impact as the company lays out how disjointed systems create all sorts of hidden costs dealers never realized they had. Ultimately this leads to a portrait of a world-class solution and a review of how Dealer Services' unique capabilities can provide that solution better than anyone else. It's a classic case of leading to, not with.

Dealers love the seminars because they deliver exactly what's advertised: actionable, valuable insight that they can immediately employ to save money, including a set of specific signs to watch out for to tell when money is being wasted in their organization. From the customer's perspective, the fact that ADP Dealer Services happens to have a solution available to help make good on the promise of that insight is almost more of a happy coincidence. This kind of support is not only hugely valuable to customers, it's hugely appreciated. It makes the seminar memorable and significantly sets ADP Dealer Services apart from the competition in the minds of its customers.

And the results of that kind of differentiation through Commercial Teaching have been staggering. In a year when new car sales in the U.S. were down 40 percent, ADP Dealer Services' revenue was down only 4 percent. Did they hit their growth goals? Well, in a way, yes, given what happened to the auto industry across those three years. But more important, at a time when the only possible path to growth was to increase one's piece of the ever-shrinking pie, Dealer Services did that and then some.

But just as important, they won the battle not only of market share but of "mind share," significantly reinforcing their role in the industry as the best source for quality, market-leading insight. All because they shifted from talking to customers about ADP Dealer Services' business to talking to customers about *their* business. More recently, Theresa Russel, head of Dealer Services' sales operations, told us, "Even with the improvement in sales throughout the automotive retail industry of late, the information we provide in these seminars continues to resonate. Whether dealers need to survive or—better still—grow their business, they are still looking for interesting ways to better manage their businesses, and that's exactly what the seminars provide."

It's a fantastic example of Commercial Teaching: The single biggest incremental opportunity to drive growth isn't in the products and services you sell, but in the quality of the insight you deliver as part of the sale itself.

6

TAILORING FOR RESONANCE

WHY DOES THIS idea of tailoring show up in the data as one of the defining attributes of the Challenger rep? We believe this has to do with the increase in consensus buying (i.e., the need to have the broader organization on board before moving ahead with a purchase) that's arisen as a reaction to the push to sell more complex solutions to customers. The data bears this out and suggests that this isn't just reps complaining, it's the new reality of solution selling. Yes, the recent financial crisis and economic downturn exacerbated customer risk aversion, but the increase in consensus requirements is a trend we were tracking long before the downturn.

WHAT DECISION MAKERS REALLY WANT

Earlier we discussed the findings from our customer loyalty survey—specifically, that 53 percent of B2B customer loyalty is a product of how you sell, not what you sell. One of the fascinating things we were able to do in that survey was to split out decision makers from influencers and end users in order to understand what makes these two different types of stakeholders loyal to a certain supplier.

Let's look first at decision makers—defined in our study as the people who actually sign the agreement. These individuals generally fall into one of two categories: senior executives or procurement. So what really matters to these senior buyers?

When we isolate decision makers from the rest of the sample, and then compare the impact of the overall sales experience with that of the individual rep selling into the account, what we find is that for decision makers, aspects of the overall sales experience are *nearly twice* as important as individual rep attributes. Decision makers think of themselves as buying from organizations, not from individuals. So what does that mean for your sales organization?

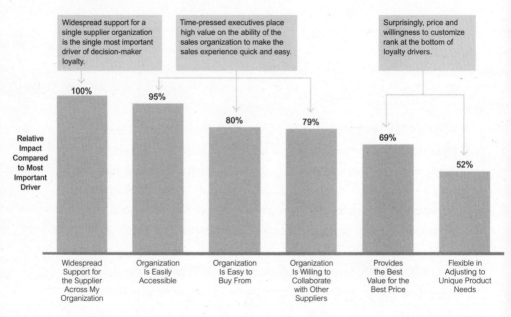

Source: CEB, CEB Sales Leadership Council, 2011.

Figure 6.1. Sales Experience Drivers of Customer Loyalty for Decision Makers (Indexed)

Of all the things that decision makers care about, topping the list in figure 6.1 is "widespread support for the supplier across my organization." One way to think of that is that senior decision makers simply aren't willing to go out on a limb for a supplier on a big purchase—at least not on their own.

At the same time, we found that decision makers don't want you to waste their time, either. They want suppliers to be accessible, easy to buy from, and willing to collaborate with other suppliers when necessary.

Finally, while we might have assumed that things like price and willingness to customize would top the list for decision makers, they're significantly less important than widespread support and ease of doing business.

That's a hugely important finding and flies in the face of most sales training that emphasizes the need to identify and engage the C-level buyer. Your reps spend so much time and effort trying to go directly to the senior decision maker, thinking, "If we can just get in that door, that's going to help us close the deal." But the best path to the decision maker isn't directly through that door at all. It turns out it's an *indirect* path that a rep needs to take to earn that decision maker's support, one that lays the groundwork with the customer's team—identifying, nurturing, and encouraging key customer stakeholders across the organization.

When it does come time to decide, the decision maker wants to know he's got the strong backing of his team. In other words, the consensus sale isn't something you should be fighting—it's something you should be actively *pursuing*. You can't just elevate the conversation and cut everyone else out because it's exactly that team input that the decision maker values most when it comes to loyalty.

One final point: When we broke out senior executives and compared them side by side with procurement for what makes them loyal, we found almost no difference between the two groups. Not surprisingly, senior execs place higher value on rep knowledge, and procurement places greater value on reps' not overstating the value of their product, but that's about it. Both groups prioritize widespread support and ease of use above any significant differences.

If loyalty at the senior level is all about winning widespread support from the team, then you're going to need to understand how to generate that widespread support. You need to know what drives loyalty for the team, not just seniormost decision makers.

THE KEY TO GENERATING "WIDESPREAD SUPPORT"

Just as we did with decision makers, we can look at what it is that drives loyalty for end users and influencers—those individuals who play a key role in a purchase but don't ultimately sign the check. Managed well, these individuals are powerfully positioned to advocate on your behalf.

First, when we isolate influencers and end users from the larger sample, and compare the impact on their loyalty of the overall sales experience versus that of the individual rep, what we find is that—unlike decision makers—these influencers place *much* more emphasis on the individual rep selling to them. End users don't think of themselves as buying from organizations; they buy from people. So what is it about the people they interact with that makes them more likely to be loyal?

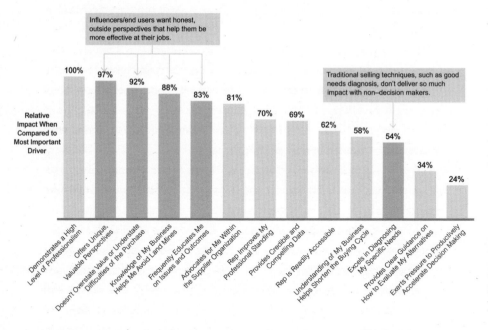

Source: CEB, CEB Sales Leadership Council, 2011.

Figure 6.2. Drivers of Sales Representative Loyalty for Influencers and End Users (Indexed)

As you look at figure 6.2, you'll notice that the biggest driver of end-user and influencer loyalty is the rep's professionalism. Most likely, this is the legacy of years of reps overpromising and underdelivering. You remember the increased customer skepticism we talked about earlier? This is where it's gotten you. Customers are simply looking for a professional—someone they can believe, and someone they can trust. As one member put it, "We want our customers to think of our reps as an extension of their own organization . . . to view them as a resource and not just a nuisance." We really think it's that kind of professionalism that customers are thinking about here.

But the bigger story lies in the next set of drivers we found, right behind professionalism in their predictive power: the ability of the rep to "offer unique and valuable perspectives" and "frequently educate the customer on issues and outcomes." In other words, what you find is a whole set of high-scoring loyalty drivers around the rep's ability to help non–decision makers recognize previously underappreciated or under-valued needs.

Contrary to conventional wisdom, more traditional selling skills like needs analysis are much farther down the list when it comes to driving end-user and influencer loyalty. So while sales organizations continue to pour time and money into helping reps to ask better, more incisive questions, these skills prove to be *much* more weakly associated with loyalty, as customers aren't looking for reps to anticipate, or "discover," needs they already know they have, but rather to *teach* them about op-portunities to make or save money that they didn't even know were possible.

What the data tells us is that for non–decision makers, loyalty is *much less* about discovering needs they already know, and much more about teaching them something they don't know, for example, something new about how to compete more effectively in their world. Customers will repay you with loyalty when you teach them something they value, not just sell them something they need. Remember, it's not just the products and services you sell, it's the insight you deliver as part of the sales in-teraction itself.

When you think about it, these findings provide a very clear road map for turning influencers and end users into actual advocates for your organization. This is how you build the widespread support that decision makers are looking for—by teaching end users something of value.

Yet while a teaching approach presents a huge untapped opportunity for managing customer stakeholders more strategically than you have in the past, *nearly two-thirds* of suppliers report using customer stakeholder interactions to extract insight, rather than provide it. As you might have guessed, most reps spend their time mining influencers for more information on decision-making processes and priorities, rather than empowering their potential stakeholders with valuable insight they can take back to their organizations.

In fact, ask yourself this: How does *your* sales organization currently manage stakeholders and influencers? How likely is it that these influencers would find interactions with your sales reps to be valuable and memorable? Would they use words like "interesting," "new," "thought-provoking," or "game-changing" to describe their conversations with your salespeople? Do your reps deliver value in every interaction? If you're anything like most sales organizations, the answer is probably no.

Lest we leave you with the impression that insight is something only valued by customer stakeholders, it is worth noting that this strategy isn't lost on executive-level decision makers either.

Yes, these senior buyers care most about widespread support, but as business leaders, they are just as interested in new ideas to save money or make money as their teams are. Figure 6.3 shows the overlap in loyalty drivers between decision makers and end users. It turns out that a teaching approach is an opportunity that serves a sales organization well regardless of whom reps are engaging with.

Senior decision makers don't want their own time wasted nor do they want salespeople to waste the time of others in the organization—they want widespread support before pulling the trigger on a purchase, but they won't let a rep go out to build that support if the rep doesn't have something compelling to share. Similarly, in sales efforts that start farther down in the organization—with the end users themselves—these individuals are highly unlikely to grant you access to their bosses unless they are supremely confident that you will add value once you sit down with them.

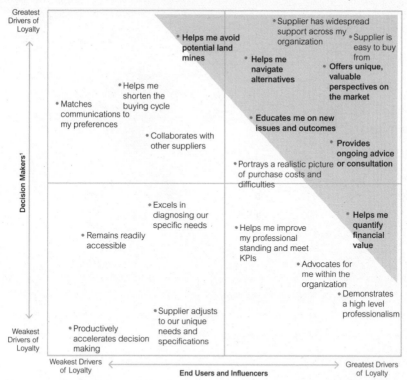

¹ From a statistical perspective, senior executives and procurement officials evaluate the purchase experience in almost identical terms.
Source: CEB, CEB Marketing Leadership Council, 2011 CEB; CEB Sales Leadership Council, 2011.

Figure 6.3. Purchase Experience Loyalty Drivers for Decision Makers Versus End Users and Influencers

THE NEW PHYSICS OF SALES

When you put all this data together, it has far-reaching consequences for sales effectiveness. One of the conventional strategies for building loyalty is to elevate the conversation to the C-suite. But of all the things that decision makers could care about when it comes to doing business with a particular supplier, the most important thing, as you now know, is that the supplier has "widespread support across the organization."

You can see implications of that finding mapped out dramatically in figure 6.4 (page 108). In the traditional approach, reps pull information from customer stakeholders in order to present the senior decision maker with a more finely tuned pitch. The link between stakeholders and

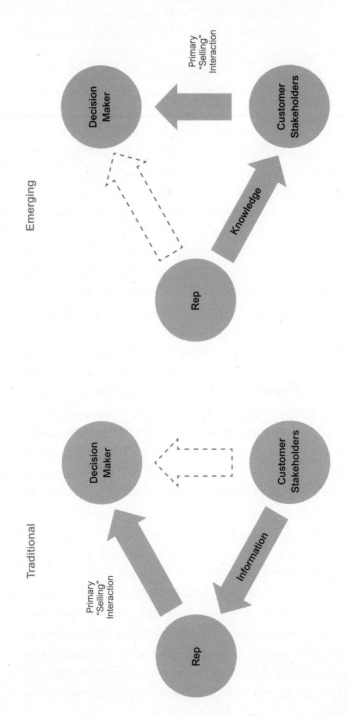

Figure 6.4. The New Physics of Sales

Source: CEB, CEB Sales Leadership Council, 2011.

decision makers is perceived as relatively weak, compared with the relationship the rep can establish directly with the decision maker, so information largely flows clockwise from advocate to rep to decision maker.

The emerging model, however, flows in the opposite direction: The best way you sell more stuff over time isn't by going directly to the person who signs the deal, but by approaching him or her *indirectly* through stakeholders able to establish more widespread support for your solution. The link between stakeholders and the decision maker is significantly stronger, whereas the link between the rep and the decision maker is significantly weaker—the rep's ability to influence the sale in the executive suite is nowhere near as strong as stakeholders' ability to do the same thing.

However, just as important as the *direction* of the information flow is the *nature* of the actual information flowing through them. In the traditional model, it's customer-generated intelligence valuable to the supplier. In the emerging model, it's supplier-generated insight valuable to the customer. This is the new physics of sales—it's like the whole world is spinning in the opposite direction. And this shift begs an important question. Over the last several years, how well have you balanced the time, effort, and money you've invested in gaining access to the customer's executive office with comparable efforts to identify key stakeholders and equip them to evangelize on your behalf? For most organizations, that's a huge missed opportunity. While you shouldn't stop calling on decision makers, you now know that those efforts do not negate the huge impact key stakeholders can have on driving more business over time. And this is something your best sales reps, your Challengers, do as a matter of course.

TAILORING THE MESSAGE

From a practical standpoint, what all of this means is that your reps now have to talk to more people than ever just to get the deal done. And we have found that one of the biggest obstacles that core reps grapple with when it comes to dealing with a consensus-based buying environment is how to tailor the sales message to these different stakeholders in order to achieve maximum resonance.

For individual customers, tailoring takes on many forms. A good way to think about how to tailor messages is to start at the broadest level—the customer's industry—and to work your way down, to the person's company, the person's role, and, finally, to that individual person. Figure 6.5, which is used in the CEB Challenger Development Program, shows these progressive "layers" of tailoring:

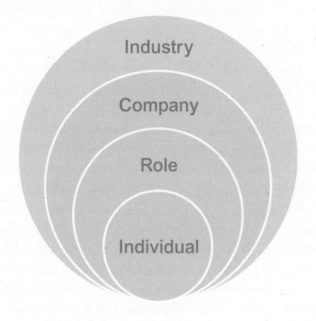

Source: CEB, CEB Sales Leadership Council, 2011.

Figure 6.5. Layers of Tailoring

As you look at that diagram, think about how well your current sales approach resonates at each of these levels for each of the many diverse customer stakeholders your reps now need to contact. The vast majority of sales messaging out in the market is not contextualized at *any* level let alone at each of these levels for each kind of stakeholder. Typically, that messaging is about a supplier and that supplier's product and services.

So as a starting point, marketing can add a tremendous amount of value simply by helping sales reps to tailor at the industry and company levels. There are so many sources of information—and many of them free—that can aid a rep in offering, at the very least, some industry and company context to the sales pitch. What's going on in terms of industry trends and current events? Has a big competitor recently folded or has there been a meaningful merger? Is the customer rapidly gaining or losing share? What about regulatory changes? What do the company's recent press releases and earnings statements suggest about strategic priorities?

When a rep comes in not just with a sales pitch, but with a sense of what's going on in that customer's company and industry, you've got the beginnings of a tailored message. These outer two layers are arguably the easier ones, and when you see tailored messaging in practice, it's usually at this level. Much rarer is messaging that is tailored at the level of a customer stakeholder's role—and rarer still is messaging that's tailored *to that individual,* i.e., their personal goals and objectives.

REDUCING VARIABILITY

Many sales leaders think of the ability to tailor to individual stakeholders as some sort of supernatural ability found only among their very best salespeople. For the rest of the sales force, the biggest obstacle to tailoring—companies assume—is their core reps' natural lack of empathy, sensitivity, or listening skills. But that's not the case. The biggest challenge to getting tailoring right is that it seems there are *so many* different things reps need to know to tailor effectively. So if you call on new people at the customer and you want to make sure you deliver as tailored a message as possible, what do you focus on? Their personality type? Their role? Their region? Their interests? The list of possibilities seems endless. So how do you narrow it down? How do you get from that amorphous cloud to a tailored, resonant message?

As you'll recall from chapter 2, two things Challenger reps tailor to are their knowledge of an individual stakeholder's value drivers and an understanding of the economic drivers of that person's business. A Challenger rep arrives at the customer with a deep understanding of how individual stakeholders fit into their overall business—what their role is and what they are worried about—as well as the specific quantifiable results that those individuals want to achieve.

Challenger reps aren't focused on what they are selling, but on what the person they're speaking to is trying to accomplish. Most sales reps tend to deliver the same message whether they're talking to senior decision makers or more junior end users, and usually that message is about your products rather than the customer's challenges.

So how do you get your entire sales force to tailor their approach to each individual stakeholder's most pressing needs? Let's look at some tailoring tools that can help reps speak to individuals in their language about their context and outcomes.

Customer outcomes are what an individual at the customer organization is trying to achieve—how they would define success as part of their job.

These outcomes encompass the actual activity or responsibility in need of improvement, the metric used to measure that task, and the direction and magnitude of the desired change. Examples of outcome statements might include, "Decrease reject rate by 5 percent on our high-capacity production line," or "Decrease the number of clicks it takes for customers to find an answer on our Web site."

There are some significant benefits to approaching a customer's needs in this way. First, customer outcomes are predictable, especially in terms of a customer's role. If you can figure out what CIOs at five different companies care about, chances are you can use that information to predict what other CIOs at similar companies care about as well. Second, these outcomes typically remain fairly stable across time and people. If a CIO gets promoted, her successor will probably have similar goals. Third, for any given role, they're finite. In other words, you can develop a short list of desired outcomes and focus on the few things that that person cares about most. And lastly, the approach is scalable. Once you've learned it, you can apply the same concept again and again across a company's org chart.

The best thing about understanding and mapping customer outcomes is that you don't have to rely on individual reps to figure all this out on their own. This is something that can be determined centrally—in marketing or sales operations—and then given to your reps in the form of a tool.

Solae, a maker of soy-based food ingredients, has done just that. This company has found a way to focus reps' conversations with various customer stakeholders on the specific capabilities and messages that will resonate most strongly with that individual.

TAILORING CASE STUDY: SOLAE'S MESSAGE-TO-ROLE MAPPING

Recently, Solae launched an aggressive strategy to sell bigger, more complex solutions in order to grow their market beyond traditional applications. As has been the experience of most companies that shift from selling products to selling solutions, these efforts brought a much wider range of stakeholders into each deal than had previously been the case. Solae's sales team was now talking to CMOs, VPs of manufacturing, procurement officers, and anyone else with a stake in their solution.

This was a big change for Solae's sales reps. However, the real problem was that reps led off these conversations with the same product and technical specifications they had used with the technical experts they had more traditionally dealt with in the past. But more often than not these newer stakeholders had no idea what the Solae reps were talking about. The rep might as well have been speaking a foreign language. Many of these nontechnical stakeholders would scratch their heads and say, "So what?" once the Solae rep was finished delivering the pitch. These customers couldn't make a connection between all of the technical specifications of Solae's products and what was most important to them. And that—as you can imagine—significantly hampered the company's solutions strategy.

Framing the Personal Win

To boost reps' ability to approach various customer stakeholders in a language they were more likely to understand, Solae's first step was to document for the rep what these various customer stakeholders cared about in the first place. To do that they went beyond general demographic information, providing their reps with a set of cards explaining what each stakeholder was trying to accomplish as a business leader. In

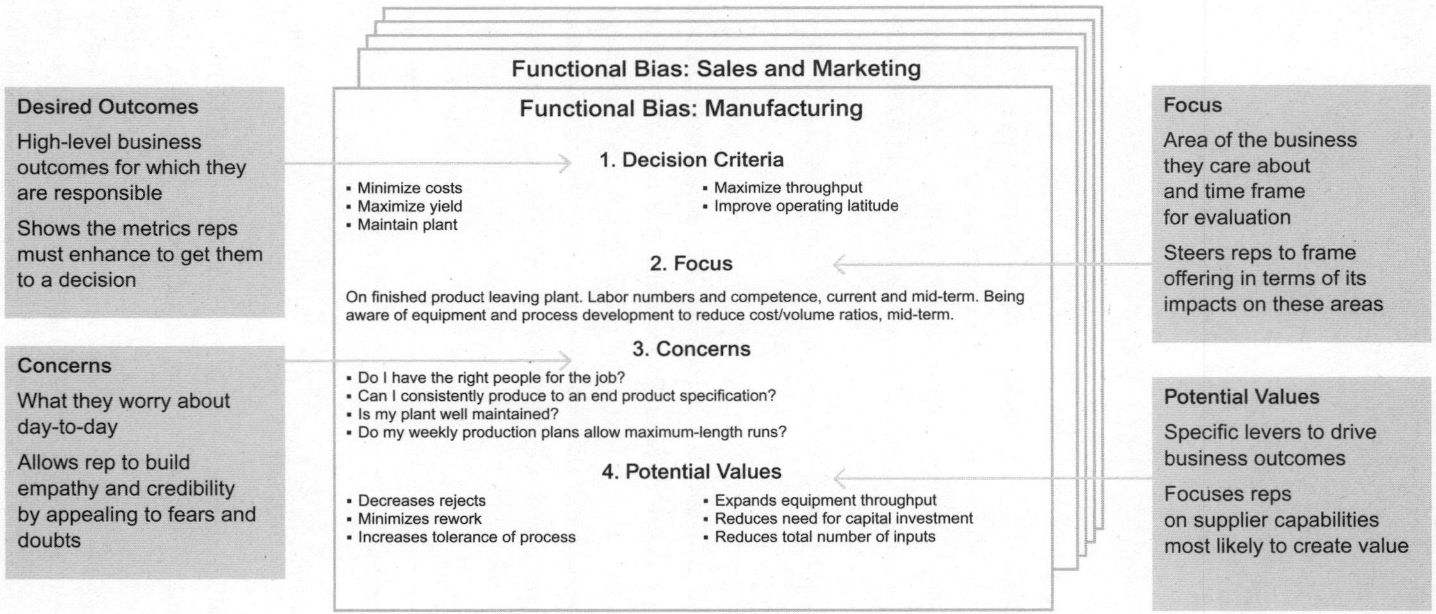

Functional Bias: Sales and Marketing

Functional Bias: Manufacturing

Desired Outcomes

High-level business outcomes for which they are responsible

Shows the metrics reps must enhance to get them to a decision

1. Decision Criteria

- Minimize costs
- Maximize yield
- Maintain plant
- Maximize throughput
- Improve operating latitude

Focus

Area of the business they care about and time frame for evaluation

Steers reps to frame offering in terms of its impacts on these areas

2. Focus

On finished product leaving plant. Labor numbers and competence, current and mid-term. Being aware of equipment and process development to reduce cost/volume ratios, mid-term.

Concerns

What they worry about day-to-day

Allows rep to build empathy and credibility by appealing to fears and doubts

3. Concerns

- Do I have the right people for the job?
- Can I consistently produce to an end product specification?
- Is my plant well maintained?
- Do my weekly production plans allow maximum-length runs?

Potential Values

Specific levers to drive business outcomes

Focuses reps on supplier capabilities most likely to create value

4. Potential Values

- Decreases rejects
- Minimizes rework
- Increases tolerance of process
- Expands equipment throughput
- Reduces need for capital investment
- Reduces total number of inputs

Figure 6.6. Components of Functional Bias

Source: CEB, CEB Sales Leadership Council, 2011.

sum, each explains a stakeholders' functional bias: their personal value drivers and their economic context.

The example functional bias card in figure 6.6 is for a head of manufacturing. On these functional bias cards, you find things like the high-level decision criteria (or business outcomes) that a person in this role cares most about. Reps also get a sense of the stakeholder's focus, or those things that that person monitors most often in order to achieve the high-level outcomes in the first section. In addition, the tool captures a stakeholder's key concerns—the questions that that person asks day-to-day to do the job, the things they worry about most. This is incredibly fertile ground for building empathy and credibility. And lastly, the tool captures for reps the stakeholder's potential value areas. These are the levers this person might pull to improve performance. So if a sales rep is going to tailor the solution to this person's desired outcomes, these are the types of things that that solution is going to have to do. This is the language you use to sell your solution to this particular person.

This is how you translate customer insight into something reps can actually use to tailor. With information like this, reps don't need to ask the customer the dreaded "What's keeping you up at night?" question, because they already know. It's right there on the card. It's a clear, easy-to-use framework for each major stakeholder's context and outcomes, all laid out in a powerful but user-friendly format.

Getting Past the "So What"

That said, in addition to the customer outcomes cards, Solae provides reps with very specific guidance on how to position each of its primary solutions, or product bundles, to different people across the customer organization.

Here is where Solae makes tailoring very concrete. This is exactly the kind of help reps need to adopt more of a Challenger rep posture. What you see in figure 6.7 is a hypothetical tailoring tool for Solae's "Solution A" (some of the information is disguised here, given its proprietary nature). Solae uses the tool to show reps the various customer stakeholders who are relevant for Solution A, as well as the high-level outcomes most

CUSTOMER RELEVANCE				SOLUTION B
CUSTOMER RELEVANCE				SOLUTION A

Function	Marketing	Purchasing
Functional Needs/Desired Outcomes	• Increase sales • Increase market share • Build brand image • Expand market offerings	• Minimize inventory • Consistent supply • Minimize overall costs • Supplier relationships
Our Capabilities and Value	**Sustainability claims** *Lorem ipsum dolor sit amet, consectetur adipiscing elit. Donec quis quam. Nullam in odio. Pellentesque consectetur.*	**Inventory management** *Aenean pellentesque. Cras mauris. Suspendisse ultrices, arcu ac faucibus dictum, ante urna placerat nisi, eget lobortis eros erat molestie purus.*
	Consumer insight *Pellentesque habitant morbi tristique senectus et netus et malesuada fames ac turpis egestas. Phasellus lacinia mollis velit.*	**Reduce overall spend** *In magna. Pellentesque ullamcorper metus. Lorem ipsum dolor sit amet, consectetur adipiscing elit. Donec a sapien eu turpis iaculis gravida.*

Source: Solae LLC; CEB, CEB Sales Leadership Council, 2011.

Figure 6.7. Desired Outcomes and Supplier Capabilities Mapped to Functional Roles

important to each of those individuals. The tool also shows the primary means by which that person is likely to achieve those outcomes—for instance, increase sales, increase market share, or build brand image. Finally, in the real version of the tool, Solae offers its reps some specific "scripting" tying Solae's Solution A directly back to what that individual is looking to achieve. This scripting isn't meant to be delivered verbatim. Rather, it's meant to serve as a set of "conversational guidelines" to direct the rep to the specific language that will resonate most strongly with that individual.

This is tailoring at its best. Using it, a rep will be speaking to the customer in their own language about how to better achieve the outcomes that they care about most in their context. This is also the kind of thing that Challengers might do instinctively, but that the majority of reps struggle with mightily—and that's really the beauty of a tool like this: It's a tailoring "cheat sheet" to help the rest of their reps sound more like the ones who do this well. It's simple, it's concrete, and it's based on context and outcomes. What's more, it provides managers with a way to scale tailoring across the sales organization.

MAKING TAILORING HAPPEN

Still, to ensure that that tailored message remains front and center with each customer stakeholder through the entire sales process, Solae goes one step further. Once a deal has progressed far enough along the sales process, and the Solae account team has developed a project proposal for customer review, their reps use a template similar to the one you see in figure 6.8 to both win and document customer buy-in to the project.

Stage 3: Account Team Develops Project

		Sales/Marketing	Manufacturing	Technical/R&D	Purchasing
Necessary Conversations	**Customer name:** Kent & Company				
	Overall project objective	Improve customer margins through cost reductions to justify relationship expansion • **Customer gets:** Lengthened end product life • **Customer gets:** Reduced production intensity			
	Functional needs relative to project objective	Maintain or improve end product quality during cost cuts	Reduce production energy intensity and plant wear and tear	Ensure our components meet regulations	Maintain or reduce total spending on inputs
	Key constraints that could derail the project	Consumers perceive products using our input in negative light			
	Our capabilities to overcome derailers/support objectives	Consumer insight: • Test out formulations • Co-marketing			
	Account's method of measurement	• Net promoter score • Churn rate			

Stage 4: Supplier Commits Resources to Project Execution

Source: Solae LLC; CEB, CEB Sales Leadership Council, 2011.

Figure 6.8. Value Planning Tool as Stage-Gate Between Project Development and Execution

The template captures the agreed-upon high-level project objective—laid out specifically in terms of what the customer gets and the major stakeholders across whom Solae needs to build consensus. Then, for each stakeholder, Solae documents the specific outcome that the proposed solution addresses for that individual. For example, for marketing, the goal is to "maintain or improve product quality and taste despite cutting costs." And then, for each role, Solae documents in writing that person's strongest concern or objection and the specific capabilities or actions Solae will employ to overcome those objections.

The most impressive thing about this approach is that *all* of this is mapped out *with* the customer. This information is determined through conversations and then captured using the tool. Though it's not required, Solae's very best reps actually ask that stakeholder to *sign off* on the column indicating their agreement with the plan. That way each stakeholder is agreeing, in advance, to the value you're going to create for them as an individual and how that value is going to be measured across the life of the deal. As a result, when it comes time for this person to decide whether or not they're going to support the deal, they're not making that decision based on some vague sense of whether the deal is "good for the company." Instead, they can look at this sheet and see exactly how it's tailored to their specific goals. And you can imagine what happens when the rep ultimately sits down with the top-level decision maker to close the deal and he can lay this document on the table. There's your consensus right there—all captured on a single piece of paper.

In fact, even if you use it only for internal purposes, this tool still represents an essential and yet typically missing page in any good account plan: a concrete, concise summary of how you're going to deliver your solution in a way that doesn't just meet overall expectations, but individual ones as well. In the end, Solae's approach represents a simple yet elegant means to capture on paper what your Challenger reps do in their heads every day—address each customer *stakeholder* as if he or she actually was *the customer*. Because in today's world of consensus-based selling, that's exactly who stakeholders are.

7

TAKING CONTROL OF THE SALE

SO FAR, WE'VE checked off two of the three key attributes of the Challenger profile, teaching and tailoring. Our next stop is a look at the third distinguishing characteristic of Challenger reps: their ability to take control of the sale.

According to the data, this ability comes from two things: Challenger reps are naturally more comfortable talking about money, and they're able to "push" the customer. What we're really talking about here is the Challenger's ability to demonstrate and hold firm on value and the ability to maintain momentum across the sales process. Challengers are comfortable discussing money because they are confident in the value they will provide to the customer. There's really nothing that instills confidence like knowing that you will deliver superior value to your customers—and Challengers have that confidence in spades. This means that the Challenger has no problem respectfully pushing back when the customer asks for a discount, looser terms, or increased scope without a commensurate increase in price (i.e., "freebies").

Remember, the value that the Challenger provides is built on the Commercial Teaching message. This isn't the same confidence one feels knowing their company's products and services are number one in the market. It's confidence built on the knowledge that you've *taught* the customer about a problem they didn't previously know they had. There's now a burning platform—one you created—and it just so happens that you sell the only solution to that problem. Being number one in the market is great, but unfortunately it isn't anything your customers really care about.

Challengers also create momentum. Their deals don't get stuck nearly as often in "no-decision land" the way typical core reps' deals tend to. This is because a Challenger will push things along, always thinking ahead to the next step. When Relationship Builders come to the end of a customer meeting, they won't push hard on next steps for fear of ruining what was otherwise a positive interaction. But Challengers understand that the goal is to sell a deal, not just have a good meeting; they are focused on moving ahead. This is also closely tied to the Commercial Teaching pitch. You've created momentum because you've created urgency around a previously unknown—or perhaps undervalued—opportunity or problem. Now it's time to press. Sounds straightforward enough, right?

As any sales leader knows, these things (i.e., comfort discussing money, pressuring the customer) are easier said than done for the average sales rep. That's why Challengers can be so hard to find. As human beings, our natural inclination is to seek closure, not postpone it, to reduce tension, not increase it. For sales reps, this translates into a tendency to agree with the customer, not present a different—and potentially unsettling— point of view. Yet Challenger reps have learned to do just that.

Yet given our natural propensities as people, how in the world do you increase the willingness and ability of your sales reps—especially those reps most predisposed to reducing tension, your Relationship Builders— to take control? In this chapter, we'll show you some very practical approaches to helping reps understand the best ways of taking control. But first, let's explore this notion of taking control in more depth.

THREE MISCONCEPTIONS ABOUT TAKING CONTROL

We've spent a fair bit of time earlier dispelling false notions around some of the concepts in the Challenger Selling Model, but nowhere is there more confusion than around the idea of taking control. We generally encounter three main misconceptions:

1. Taking control is synonymous with negotiation.
2. Reps only take control regarding matters of money.
3. Reps will become too aggressive if we tell them to "take control."

Let's take these one at a time. First, the common perception—given that the data suggests that Challengers are comfortable discussing money—is that taking control is synonymous with negotiation and that it is typically done at the *end* of the sales process. This couldn't be further from the truth.

Misconception #1: Taking Control Is Synonymous with Negotiation

One of the biggest misconceptions about taking control is that it's about negotiation skills. But our research shows that Challegers take control across the entirety of the sales process, not just at the end. In fact, one of the prime opportunities for taking control is actually right at the beginning of the sale.

Challengers know many sales opportunities that appear viable on the surface are little more than veiled "verification efforts" by a customer. In other words, they are cases in which the customer has already chosen a vendor to partner with, but feels the need to do some due diligence—to make sure they're getting the best deal they can—so they entertain conversations with other vendors even though they have little intention of changing their minds. In cases like this, which our research shows can be nearly 20 percent of all sales opportunities, the customer will assign a more junior member of their organization to field an RFP and meet with other possible vendors. But again, because the customer has no intention of actually buying from these other suppliers, they only allow reps to meet with the junior contact, never permitting access to more senior decision makers.

For most reps, this isn't seen as a problem. In fact, most reps *love* these opportunities. What's not to love? After all, the customer *called us*!

The typical rep response is to continue to spend time with the junior contact in the hopes of turning that individual into an advocate, eventually clawing one's way into the corner office. What we often hear from reps is something along the lines of, "We know money is going to be spent if there is an RFP out there, so it's stupid for us to not put ourselves into consideration—we at least have a chance!"

But even in this early stage of the sale, Challengers know better. They sniff out these "foils" immediately and press the contact for expanded access in exchange for continued dialogue. When these contacts don't grant the access Challenger reps know will be critical to completing the sale, their response is to cut the sales effort short and move on to the next opportunity. It seems so counterintuitive to the average rep—after all, you've got a customer that has put an RFP out for a solution you can provide, so you know there's funding for the purchase. They've also agreed to meet with the rep, and customer face time is so hard to get these days. Why would you ever want to walk away from a situation like this? But that's exactly what a Challenger does. Challenger reps know their time is better spent elsewhere.

One of our members, a global business services provider, has institutionalized this Challenger behavior across its entire sales force. This company teaches its reps to push for expanded access right from the get-go. Since much of their business is done through RFPs, they are almost always starting their sales conversations with lower-level functionaries within the customer organization, often in procurement. They tell their reps that an early litmus test of how serious a given customer is about partnering is whether they will agree to grant the supplier's sales rep access to key stakeholders. It's proven to be a remarkably accurate "tell" for a customer's real intentions and has helped the company's reps to avoid wasting time.

Their reps are taught, at the close of the first interaction, to say, "You know, typically when we engage with a customer for this sort of solution, we need certain key executives to be involved in the purchase decision. Is that the case here?" When the customer says yes, the rep asks when she'll be able to meet with those individuals. If the contact hems and haws or gives an unclear answer, the rep pushes and explains that if they can't guarantee time with those key leaders, she'll be unable to check that everybody is aligned on the value of the solution, and therefore it doesn't make sense to continue engaging in further discussions.

Neil Rackham shared with us a similar story from his research. "A big problem," he explained to us, "is the customer who invites a salesperson to come in, analyze a problem, and generate creative solutions. Many sales organizations will spend well into the six figures to pursue a complex opportunity. All too often, though, the customer encourages this free consulting work until the best solution becomes clear, at which point they go shopping for the cheapest supplier."

This is a core difference between Relationship Builders and Challengers, in Neil Rackham's assessment. "In my own research, I saw some reps losing more customers to cheaper suppliers late in the sale because they failed to take control early on. They steered clear of having a tough conversation about the commercial side of the interaction, fearing it would damage the relationship. Other reps, however, confronted the customer early in the sale, saying, 'It's going to cost us $200K to put our best thinking into your problem. We're willing to do it, but we need some assurance that if we invest in you, you'll invest in us.' These reps had far fewer customers switch to cheaper suppliers late in the sales process."

This kind of tactic seems to be a hallmark of sales high performers. One of our recent studies revealed that while all reps start their sales efforts by mapping out stakeholders within the customer organization, core performers then move to what would seem like the logical next step—understanding needs and mapping solutions against those needs. But high performers do something very different. They extend this part of the sales process by digging into these individual stakeholders' varying goals and biases, as well as business and personal objectives. As we discussed in the tailoring chapter, they map out not just *who* the key stakeholders are, but *what* these stakeholders care about and *why* they care about these things. By doing this, the Challenger is in a much better position to be able to take control right from the beginning.

Challengers find many other opportunities to take control during the sale—again, well in advance of arriving at the negotiating table. Even if a rep *can* successfully verify a customer's real intentions at the beginning of the sales process, many deals will get bogged down nevertheless. Challengers distinguish themselves by building momentum within the customer organization—momentum that enables them to drive to a conclusion faster than the typical rep.

In our interactions with Challenger reps, it's clear that they have a better-than-average appreciation for how hard it is to buy from their companies in general. This complexity in the buying process has less to do with bureaucratic hurdles suppliers put in the way of customers—though that surely is an issue in many companies—but with the fact that customers often don't know how to buy. Of course, customers don't lack the basic know-how of buying a complex solution from a supplier, but standard purchasing processes and protocols break down when every solution is unique, touching different parts of the organization.

Average reps see this complexity too, but their tendency—especially for Relationship Builders—is to "learn and react." They let the customer (who, again, is likely to be confused by the complexity of purchasing the solution) take the lead. Better to defer to the customer than to rock the boat. The rep asks questions about whom to get involved and what steps to take, but the customer is as lost as the rep.

Challengers, by contrast, "lead and simplify." Rather than assuming that the customer knows how to execute the purchase of a complex solution—which can be a faulty assumption when it comes to solution selling—they *teach the customer how to buy* the solution. They extrapolate from past successful sales efforts and apply what they've learned to help the customer work through their purchase process. Instead of asking, "Who needs to be involved?" Challenger reps *coach the customer* on who should be involved.

Sounds familiar, doesn't it? The Commercial Teaching approach, as you recall, is about getting away from the "What's keeping you up at night?" question and instead bringing unique insight to the customer about what should be keeping them up at night. It's the same idea here.

None of this is to suggest that taking control doesn't happen at the end of the sale, when both parties are sitting across from each other at the negotiating table. Of course it happens there. We know from the data that Challengers shine in negotiation settings. In fact, we'll study this very thing in more depth when we look at a negotiation training best practice from DuPont later in this chapter. That being said, it's a mistake to equate "taking control" with "negotiating." It is far more accurate to think of the latter as a small, albeit important, subset of the former.

What's more, a Challenger knows that the average sales rep will seek to take control only at the end of the sale—at the negotiating table—and so Challengers differentiate themselves by taking control from the start. Customers value this because they see the Challenger as a confident partner in the sales process, not a nervous rep crossing their fingers in the hope of making a sale.

Misconception #2: Reps Take Control Regarding Only Matters of Money

The data tells us that Challengers are "able to *push* the customer." Sure, they can push the customer on financial terms and aspects of the selling/buying process, but more important, they push the customer in terms of how they think about their world and their challenges—as well as the solution to those challenges. This is the essence of Commercial Teaching, which we discussed earlier in the book: the ability to reframe the way the customer thinks about their world.

Why is it important to take control around ideas? Because it's extremely unlikely that a customer—especially a seasoned executive—is going to roll over and accept the reframe that the Challenger delivers without a healthy does of skepticism. More likely, he'll push back. He'll ask why. He'll ask to see the supporting data. He'll say his company is different. These are the questions that make Relationship Builders' knees go weak. Seeking to defuse tension, the Relationship Builder will acquiesce, caving on the argument and hoping to salvage what's left of the conversation, in the end relegating himself to a price-driven conversation about products and survival rates rather than the bigger, more valuable solution that could have been.

But it's this kind of dialogue that the Challenger lives for. The Challenger will use constructive tension to her advantage. Instead of giving in at the first sign of resistance to her argument, the Challenger pushes back: "You're right, your company surely is different, but so are the other organizations we work with . . . and I can tell you that this insight has helped them to rethink the way they run their operations. With your permission, let's explore this idea in more depth and then circle back to make sure I've adequately addressed any concerns you might have."

Commercial Teaching puts the Challenger in a position to take control by bringing new ideas to the table—ideas the customer hadn't thought of before. But customers are savvy and conventional wisdom didn't get to be conventional by being easy to topple. There will be pushback, even if the Challenger is armed with compelling insights and supporting data. The Challenger's response when confronted with this pushback, however, is to take control of the debate.

But taking control of the debate around ideas is critical not just because it shows that the sales rep isn't going to be a pushover, but also because those ideas the Challenger brings to the table (i.e., the new problems or opportunities the rep has taught the customer to value) are directly connected to the solutions that the supplier can offer to the customer. If the rep isn't willing to convince the customer that the problem is urgent, then he won't be able to convince the customer it's worth solving.

Misconception #3: Reps Will Become Too Aggressive If We Tell Them to "Take Control"

People also confuse taking control—that is, the Challenger's tendency to be assertive during the sale—with aggressiveness. But these are actually two very different things. This is the last, but arguably most critical, misconception to address.

If we think about sales rep behavior along a spectrum, we can array it as you see in figure 7.1, with "passive" behavior on one end and "aggressive" behavior on the other.

Passive behavior, of course, is relatively self-explanatory. The rep gives in to the demands of others, uses accommodating language, and allows his personal boundaries to be breached by the customer. Sound familiar? These are the hallmarks of the Relationship Builder. The passive rep's primary goal is to *please* the customer. That desire is so powerful that

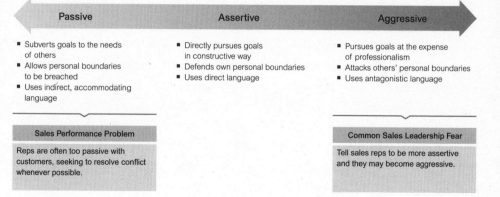

Source: CEB, CEB Sales Leadership Council, 2011.

Figure 7.1. Rep Behavior Spectrum, Passive to Aggressive

Relationship Builders will do things that are not in their best interests or in their company's best interests—for instance, proactively offering a discount when the customer hasn't even asked for one.

There's little confusion among sales leaders about what passive behavior is; the real confusion is between assertive and aggressive.

The primary difference between the two is one of posture. While aggressive people will pursue their goals by attacking others and using antagonistic language, assertive individuals are much more constructive, using strong language, perhaps, but not so strong that it's off-putting or offensive. So the rep pushes the customer, but does so with respect and sensitivity to how the customer is reacting. The rep doesn't blindly pursue his own agenda, but instead moves purposefully, always sensing and responding.

Take the example one of our members shared with us. One of his company's sales reps was selling paint to a large production line in early 2009. His company had poor margins due to the competitive environment exacerbated by rapid escalations in raw material costs. The rep for the paint supplier sent a price increase letter to purchasing and followed up with a visit to discuss the justification and to gain agreement for a price move at the beginning of the next quarter. The purchasing manager, however, flatly refused to take a price increase on the basis that business was bad (which it was). But the Challenger rep did not roll over on his price. He stood his ground during the initial visit and two others, citing the dramatically improved productivity at the paint plant due to the supplier's installed equipment and dedicated staff. Despite threats from purchasing of dire consequences for the increase (senior leadership involvement, cancellation of a long-term contract, etc.), the rep didn't cave.

The rep made an appointment with the plant manager of the facilities affected by the increase, which were also the main consumers of the paint and the beneficiaries of the service. He laid out the issue and the need for the increase. He then reviewed all of the projects that his company had completed to improve productivity at the sites. The plant manager called in his leadership team to confirm what the sales rep was telling him. They supported his value claims. The rep then asked the plant manager to set up a joint meeting with the rep and purchasing to gain support for the increase. He did so and the increase was ultimately accepted.

In this case, the rep stood his ground and was extraordinarily assertive, but not aggressive. While he was certainly close to the edge with purchasing, he made his value case and stuck with it.

Now, what's interesting about this continuum is how concerned sales leaders are that their sales reps are going to drift too far to the aggressive end of the spectrum. The general fear is that if you tell your reps to take control by being more assertive, they're going to jump over the middle of the continuum and move straight to aggressive.

But in reality, we find that almost never happens. More often than not, reps will continue to gravitate to the passive end of the continuum rather than move to the right at all. They get stuck seeking to resolve tension with the customer, rather than maintain it.

Why does this happen? First, there is a perceived power imbalance in the rep-customer relationship. Reps think that the customer has significantly more power in the relationship. Therefore, they give in to customer demands for better terms and conditions because they feel they have no choice. They often back down before they even understand fully *why* the customer is making the request! For the average rep, it's either acquiesce quickly or lose the deal. But as real as that perception may be, it turns out that reality is totally different.

A recent survey by BayGroup International of sales reps and procurement officers determined that 75 percent of reps believe that procurement has more power, while 75 percent of procurement officers believe that reps have more power! At the very least, this data tells us that if reps are giving in because they believe the customer to have more power, they're just plain wrong. Again, this is something Challenger reps seem to instinctively know. They don't back down in the sale, because they know there's always more room to negotiate than a core performer would ever believe. The Challenger just knows how to finesse—or tailor—it the right way.

We find that many sales professionals undervalue their contribution to the customer. They marginalize the tremendous value of their company's resources—not just technical expertise, but implementation and change management know-how—and overestimate the value of every objection raised by the customer. This is often an ah-ha! moment for sales reps when we deliver our Challenger training. We tell reps to think about the resources they have at their disposal to help their customers get better. To quote one of our trainers: "Think about it. You are teaching your customers things that they didn't know before. You have practical experiences from hundreds, if not thousands, of implementations, while this may be the first such implementation for your customer. Taking control means that you *know* the value of those resources and you *don't* bring them to bear willy-nilly on a customer who isn't serious about the decision. If the customer asks for a case study, or to talk to a reference, a Relationship Builder says, 'Yes!' A Challenger says, 'Sure, but let me ask you if this is the very last confirmation you need before we agree to work together and you sign the paperwork.' Why? Because the Challenger is confident in the value he and his company bring to the customer."

Another reason most reps naturally gravitate to a more passive posture is a perceived erosion of control in the supplier-customer relationship generally speaking. This is more of a temporal phenomenon, brought on by challenging economic conditions. In a tough economy, a rep is happy to take any business. The last thing they're going to do when a deal is on the table is push back on pricing. The rep just wants to get the thing closed before the customer changes their mind altogether. In difficult economic times, normally assertive reps behave more passively—and reps who are normally passive to begin with cave altogether. It's a buyer's market in large part because reps make it so by creating favorable negotiating conditions that tip the scales well into the customer's favor.

A second reason that we see reps becoming more passive with customers—and this one hits close to home—is that you've told them to act this way. How so? As it turns out, management strategies exacerbate the tendency for most reps to "go passive." If managers tell reps to focus on serving the customer and advocating for their needs—to "sit on the customer's side of the table"—this message is often interpreted by salespeople as "give the customer whatever they want."

We're hearing now more than ever before that sales leaders are urging their sales organizations to "place the customer first." The term "customer-centricity" is back in a dramatic fashion. The assumption is that if companies want to grow coming out of the recent downturn, they're going to have to ensure that everything they do delivers maximum customer value. The problem, however, is that while companies have been emphatic about their customer-centricity, they've been equally vague with their sales organizations about how to actually do that. There are several ways to be "customer-centric" that are actually *bad* for business. Two examples of this that we hear frequently from our members are discounts (or other terms and conditions that undermine profitability in exchange for little long-term gain) and assuming an order-taker posture with the customer (i.e., taking short-term orders when the customer is pushing for them, instead of getting the customer to think about longer-term business). These are things that drive companies crazy, but the messages they send out to their sales force do little to dissuade reps from the notion that these are good things to be doing for customers.

These drivers of overly passive rep behavior are the things that sales leaders need to overcome if they want to build Challenger reps capable of taking control of the sale. The real question isn't how to stop reps from being too assertive, but rather how to *get* them to be assertive enough.

EQUIPPING REPS TO TAKE CONTROL

How do companies shake reps out of their passive posture? Getting this right requires that they tackle the main obstacle that gets in the way of the average rep's being able to effectively take control: a strong desire for closure.

Reps naturally seek closure. Like most people, they are fundamentally uncomfortable with ambiguity, particularly because it's that ambiguity that typically stands between them and their commission checks. There is a natural human tendency—one that reps have to overcome—to want closure in uncomfortable situations. Succumbing to this tendency is one that absolutely kills the average rep.

Challengers, by comparison, thrive in ambiguity. They know how to navigate it and understand how it can be leveraged to their advantage. They display a remarkable level of comfort with silence during the customer conversation, as well as with keeping negotiation points and customer objections open and on the table longer than one normally would. It might be a bit of an overstatement to say they "like" tension, but it probably isn't that far from the truth.

Admittedly, this is a tough barrier to overcome. It isn't realistic to expect reps who do not like tension and ambiguity to suddenly start liking these things. At some level, this sort of response is hardwired in most of us. Either we are comfortable with these things or we aren't. And if we aren't, we'll look for any excuse to avoid them. But while you can't realistically change human behavior, you *can* help make reps aware of their natural tendencies and give them some practical tools for making sure that they don't prematurely cave when it comes to intense value discussions. This is where the DuPont practice comes in. They've developed some really smart negotiation training and tools for helping reps to avoid premature closure.

TAKING CONTROL CASE STUDY: DUPONT'S CONTROLLED NEGOTIATION ROAD MAP

As we go through the DuPont case, bear in mind that this practice focuses exclusively on taking control in negotiation settings. While Challengers take control throughout the sale, the negotiating table is still a great place to study this notion. And DuPont offers a terrific example of how to equip reps to push customers in an assertive but not aggressive manner.

Taking control is all about creating constructive tension—about challenging the way a customer sees their world, and pushing back constructively in tough negotiations. At DuPont, they've employed some powerful tools to help reps overcome their natural inclination to give in to customer demands too early in the sale. DuPont worked with negotiation training vendor BayGroup International, though it is worth noting that several vendors offer robust negotiation training products that our members have been happy with.

The goal in DuPont's case is very straightforward. This is about taking control—the third key ingredient to building Challenger reps—and an area where we can have a huge impact if we follow a recipe like this.

Purposeful Planning

DuPont is the provider of a wide range of innovative products and services sold across many industries, including agriculture, electronics, transportation, construction, and safety and protection. The key to DuPont's approach to equipping reps to take control at the negotiating table is this: You've got to have a plan. The only way that reps are going to have the confidence to not back down from challenging the customer is if they've built a strategy for doing that in advance of the sales call itself.

DuPont provides reps with a simple template for prenegotiation planning based on BayGroup International's *Situational Sales Negotiation*™ (SSN™) methodology. The SSN template itself is brief, but the range and value of information that's collected is what's critical here (see figure 7.2) as all of this information together provides powerful perspective, and puts the rep in a significantly better position when it comes time to negotiate.

This tool is all about ensuring that reps have the skills and tools to negotiate effectively rather than give in when the customer asks for concessions. The SSN template asks reps to note the relative "power positions" of the supplier—everything from products to brand, pricing, service, and relationships. The idea here is to get down on paper all of the areas in which we have relative strengths with the customer and all the ways that we have relative weaknesses. Done well, the detail in this first section alone will provide the rep with a better sense of the larger value her company brings to the table and will build the rep's confidence to demand a greater price for that value.

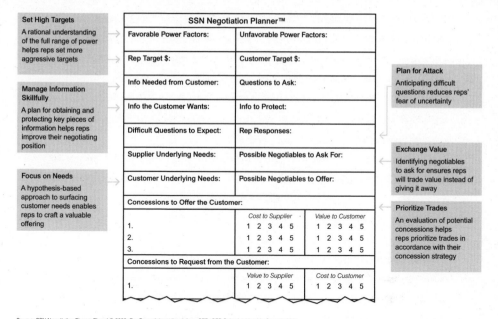

Source: SSN Negotiation Planner™ and © 2009; BayGroup International, Inc., CEB, CEB Sales Leadership Council, 2011.

Figure 7.2. Negotiation Analysis and Action Plan

The SSN template also forces DuPont reps to think in advance about all of the information they need to get from the customer and to list the specific questions they're going to ask to find those things out. Likewise, it asks the rep to detail the information the customer is likely going to want to know so that the rep is ready in the meeting to provide it or protect it, as the case may be.

Next, what difficult questions and objections is the rep likely to get from the customer and how exactly does the rep plan to respond? It's always better to prepare answers in advance, rather than be forced to come up with a response on the fly, because that almost inevitably leads to giving in way too early to customer demands. This is followed by an examination of the specific things the supplier is looking for in the deal—things they can negotiate on and a series of hypotheses around the customer's needs as well.

Finally, the SSN template asks reps to do an analysis of possible concessions to offer to the customer and concessions to request from the customer. For example, the customer might ask the rep to give in on price and the rep might ask the customer to give in on some of their customization demands. Here, the template asks the rep to score the value of those concession items for both the supplier and customer. For example, the rep might determine that offering the customer a price concession reflects a 5 in terms of cost to the supplier, perhaps because they run on very thin margins, but only a 2 to the customer in terms of value, since they're primarily concerned not with price but with the quality and workability of the product.

As you consider this planning method, ask yourself how many of your reps take the time to map out this kind of information *prior* to a negotiation, particularly one where price is likely to come up as a sticking point. Remember, winning those conversations is what really sets the Challenger apart. The Challenger rep has a scorecard like this wired into her brain. This is how she sees the world, and it's what allows her to push back on the customer when the time comes. Put another way, the SSN template is a proxy for what Challenger reps do naturally. This is how you capture the magic of Challenger rep pre-call planning and put it on one sheet of paper.

Asking your reps to use a tool like this puts you one step closer to giving them the confidence to hang tough when the conversation turns more difficult. It also forces them to play out the next few interactions in the negotiation. Our research shows that one of the biggest differentiators of high-performing reps is the amount of time they spend planning—this is a prime example. Like a great chess player, high performers are focused not just on the current move, but on the scenarios that will play out several moves ahead.

Dupont found that for most reps, being assertive takes practice and planning. This is how you put a structure around both. If you were to give this sheet to ten of your reps next week—right before they called on a customer—would they be able to fill it out? If the answer is troubling, chances are extremely good that your reps are giving in to customer demands too early because they're not equipped to push back in the moment. They're not equipped to challenge.

What else can you do to equip reps to challenge the customer's demands once they're in the sales call itself and the customer starts placing demands on the deal?

Anatomy of a Successful Negotiation

Navigating tough customer conversations is one of those things that always seems a little bit like magic. Some people just seem to be able to do it incredibly well—but it's never completely clear how. But what tangible steps can you take to help reps take control in the conversation itself?

DuPont has demystified the process by boiling it down to a four-step framework based on BayGroup International's methodology and then used the framework to put reps through a two-day *Situational Sales Negotiation* workshop focused on breaking sales reps' tendency to give in too soon.

1. Acknowledge and Defer
2. Deepen and Broaden
3. Explore and Compare
4. Concede According to Plan

Think of this as a road map for maintaining constructive tension within a negotiation. This is the kind of stuff your Challengers do naturally and the place where everyone else needs exactly this kind of concrete guidance.

How does it all work? Let's start with Acknowledge and Defer.

How do you defer a customer demand for a concession—say a price discount—without threatening the deal? Here, DuPont has done something very smart and very straightforward. They've given reps the actual words to say when that moment comes.

While it doesn't have to be verbatim, reps are encouraged to say something like, "I understand that price is something we need to address, but before we do, I'd like to take a moment to make sure I completely understand your needs—so we can make sure we're doing everything we can to make this deal as valuable as possible for you. Is that all right?"

It's a relatively simple request, but there's a lot going on here. The rep has promised closure—which the customer wants just as much as the rep—but has also won permission to proceed, assuming she gets it. And that's important, because you have to win the customer's permission to defer. If you don't, they're not going to listen to anything you say next. This is a key mistake non-Challenger reps make all the time—they rarely seek to defer at all. And if they do, it's without customer consent, which means they risk coming across as dismissive, or worse, aggressive.

Once she has permission to continue, the rep is on to the next two steps: Deepen and Broaden and Explore and Compare, which we'll examine in parallel.

At this point, the rep has bought some time but has also created some tension in the conversation. So now the rep needs a way to manage that tension and have the confidence to push forward. DuPont trains reps on a specific technique to get the deal to a better place when a customer pushes back on price. As we go through it, you'll see that what makes it so powerful is that it's a straightforward, repeatable technique that can be copied and learned by non-Challenger reps.

For Deepen and Broaden, DuPont provides reps with tactics for uncovering the customer's underlying needs, and for Explore and Compare, reps are trained on tactics for comparing and evaluating the additional needs identified during the conversation.

The primary idea here is to expand the customer's view of the things that are important to them. What else besides price matters? Maybe it's the warranty, or the service plan, or expedited shipping, or installation. Get it all out on the table so that price is no longer the only negotiable in play. During the Deepen and Broaden phase, the DuPont sales rep often starts with getting the customer to simply restate things the rep already knows the customer likes about the DuPont offering.

Once the rep has broadened that universe as much as possible, she can start to shrink it back down, coming back to price, but in a very specific manner. In this technique, reps don't run directly to "I can give you 10 percent, not 20 percent." Instead, the conversation starts with, "What are you looking to achieve with a 20 percent price reduction?" The idea is to uncover the rationale for the request, as the appropriate response will depend on that rationale.

Often the reason for the request is something that can be addressed in some other way—as it's often driven less by economic need and more by the customer's desire to achieve a specific business outcome, such as production cost reductions.

So look at what you're negotiating over now. It's not just price, but all of the other ways in which the supplier creates value for the customer and helps to solve their key challenges. Doing this, the rep has significantly expanded the options for negotiation. The rep's now in a much better place to offer concessions that are less painful to their top-line revenue—and potentially options the customer values more. As they move to comparing various trade-offs with the customer, this is where all the prep work they did with the pre-call planning tool becomes so incredibly important. If they've done their homework well, they know the cost-to-value trade-off for each one of the solution elements for their company.

This brings us to the final mile of negotiation: Concede According to Plan. This isn't just a fun play on words. Reps are taught the importance of proceeding according to a carefully planned negotiation strategy that trades away low-value solution elements first before defaulting to price. In other words, determining *what* you're willing to concede is important . . . but what is often overlooked is *how* and *when* in the negotiation those concessions should be given. There are many different ways to make concessions to a customer; each can send a very different message to the customer, even when you ultimately achieve the exact same results.

DuPont teaches their reps to avoid certain concession patterns—such as starting with small concessions and then offering bigger ones as the negotiations progress, or putting a "take it or leave it" offer on the table—because these approaches are not just risky, they can leave the customer feeling cheated. Instead they teach reps to concede negotiables in an order and an amount that ensures both parties feel they're winning. For instance, they teach reps to start with a meaningful concession and then to offer smaller and smaller concessions as negotiations continue.

Techniques like this help DuPont reps manage tension in a constructive manner. That's not something non-Challenger reps would have known how to do otherwise. The point here is to give them the information they need to make better choices when it comes to negotiation and to understand the implications and possible repercussions of employing one of these strategies versus another. This is how you set them up for success when they challenge.

To really get the feel for the difference, during the Situational Sales

Negotiation skill-building workshops DuPont reps role-play different concession patterns and then discuss how they feel when the negotiation ends. This serves to illustrate the effect that different concession patterns will have on customers and ultimately gives reps the confidence that they have a smart plan to getting to an agreement—one that will leave the customer feeling that they won, rather than that they got cheated.

A WORD OF CAUTION

While the DuPont case focuses on taking control within the negotiation phase of the sale, an earlier point in this chapter bears repeating here: Taking control happened *throughout* the sales process, not just the end of it. In our Challenger Development Program, much of the "taking control" module is not focused on negotiation at all. It's a point we really hammer home: Taking control *has to* happen throughout the sale, lest it end up feeling "fake" (or, worse, disingenuous or off-putting) to the customer.

We share several practical examples and techniques for doing this. One of the basic techniques we focus on is making powerful requests, which should be done throughout the sale. Making powerful requests helps the customer understand that the rep is here to move things forward; it is a great tool from the Challenger's "taking control" toolkit.

How does it work? Here's a quick example: A rep has showed his customer that they are wasting millions on facilities costs because of their inefficient server management. The proposed solution will save the customer a good deal of money, but others need to be involved in the purchase decision if it's to move forward. A powerful request might sound something like this: "From our discussion, we've agreed that the implementation of a rack-based server solution would save you $5 million a year. For you to reap these savings in the current fiscal year, we really need to install the new hardware soon. So to get started, I will need a signed contract from Dave by next week, which will allow us to bring the implementation engineers onsite and start the process so you can hit your savings target." This is just one example, which is focused on closing, but there are many others that help reps understand how to take control even earlier in the sales process.

PULLING IT ALL TOGETHER

Taking control is the one pillar of the Challenger Selling Model that strikes most sales leaders as more nature than nurture. But while it's true that it helps for reps to have been born with the "assertiveness gene," it is by no means a requirement for them to be successful. The solution to overcoming passivity is straightforward: Teach reps the importance of clarity of direction over quick closure, and teach them how to create real value within the sales process. When combined, these skills can help any sales rep to create a powerful proxy for natural assertiveness.

8

THE MANAGER AND THE CHALLENGER SELLING MODEL

SO FAR WE'VE focused on the rep skills and organizational capabilities required to implement the Challenger Selling Model. But anybody who's ever attempted to execute large-scale change within a sales organization will know there's one glaring omission to this story: the frontline sales manager.

As a research organization devoted to improving sales performance, we've studied nearly every topic in the sales world, and the message in the data is always the same: If you don't get frontline sales managers on board, the initiative will fail. Whether it's changes to comp plans, the CRM system, the sales process, or more basic skills and behaviors, it always comes back to the manager. The frontline sales manager in any sales organization is the fundamental link between strategy and execution—this is where change initiatives and sales force transformations live or die.

Implementing the Challenger Selling Model is no different. You cannot expect to successfully build a Challenger sales organization if your frontline sales management layer is broken. It's the linchpin in terms of making the model work. While this point may be obvious to the seasoned sales leader, what sales organizations can actually do to boost manager effectiveness is less so. While there is rather broad consensus that manager quality is the most important lever for driving rep performance, sales leaders tend to view manager effectiveness as a sort of enigma. As one of our members told us, "I know that manager success is crucial to my overall success; problem is, I don't know what to do about it."

And that concern is widespread, especially as sales leaders look to the future. In fact, when we asked our members about manager capability, a shocking 63 percent reported that their managers do not have the skills and competencies they need as their sales model evolves, to say nothing of the 9 percent of managers who don't even have the skills required to be successful in their role *currently*. Three-quarters of our members self-identify as having managers who aren't going to perform in the new environment. And that's deeply troubling. While leaders agree on the fundamental importance of the role, very few feel confident about the actual people currently occupying that role, and most are even less confident still about what to do about it.

PORTRAIT OF A WORLD-CLASS SALES MANAGER

In an effort to identify the key attributes of a world-class sales manager—the skills, behaviors, and attitudes that matter most for sales management excellence—we created a survey we call the Sales Leadership Diagnostic. At last count, more than sixty-five companies have administered this diagnostic (to more than 12,000 reps), and we have collected data on more than 2,500 individual frontline sales managers.

PARTIAL SAMPLE OF VARIABLES TESTED			
MANAGEMENT FUNDAMENTALS	SELLING	COACHING	SALES LEADERSHIP
• Maintains integrity • Displays reliability • Recognizes direct reports	• Teaches customers new insights • Tailors offers • Discusses pricing and money with customers	• Customizes coaching approach • Prepares for coaching interactions • Communicates expectations	• Maximizes territory potential • Analyzes pipeline data • Delegates projects

PARTIAL SAMPLE OF VARIABLES TESTED			
MANAGEMENT FUNDAMENTALS	**SELLING**	**COACHING**	**SALES LEADERSHIP**
• Builds cohesive teams • Practices two-way communication • Listens to and understands rep's point of view	• Maintains productive customer relationships • Is skilled at negotiation	• Shares product or industry knowledge • Follows through on development activities	• Drives the sales culture • Shares best practices • Makes trade-offs • Innovates new ways to position offers

As with any survey we conduct, the data is a strong, representative sample of every major industry, geography, and go-to-market model across our membership. In the survey, we asked reps to assess their manager's performance across sixty-four different attributes of performance, some of which you see in the four broad categories in the table on page 141 and above.

First, we asked about management fundamentals—things like integrity, reliability, recognition, and team-building skills. These variables aren't necessarily specific to sales, but they are incredibly important. So we included them in our analysis to understand how they compare to other attributes in terms of driving manager performance. Second, we looked at attributes related to actual selling ability. While we don't want our managers selling *for* their reps, it stands to reason that they probably do need to know how to sell if they're going to help others to do it better. Here, we asked about attributes like negotiation skills and whether the manager offers the customer unique perspectives. Third, we asked about the manager's coaching skills. Do managers prepare for and customize coaching interactions? Do they follow through on their development commitments? Lastly, we looked at sales-specific aspects of leadership—things like account planning, territory management, and the level of innovation the manager shows in positioning offers to customers.

Next, to ensure that we weren't allowing one unhappy rep to skew our results, we excluded those managers from the analysis for whom we had data from fewer than three reps. Then, to make the results manageable, we applied factor analysis to the data, boiling it down to the smallest possible number of statistically significant groups or categories. The factor analysis told us that those sixty-four variables fall into five distinct categories. Finally, to understand how important each category is relative to the other four, we ran a regression analysis of those factors against actual manager performance—as determined by both the reps and the companies. And that allowed us to determine, of all the things a manager *could* be good at, which of these sixty-four skills and behaviors matter most for actual manager performance— as assessed by the reps who observe those behaviors every single day as well as by companies, which have a broader sense of how those managers maintain and grow their territories over time. Ultimately, this exercise generated the answer to the key question of manager performance, i.e., the smallest number of statistically significant— and distinct—categories that, when combined, explain frontline sales manager excellence.

To interpret what we found, let's start by separating management fundamentals, like reliability, integrity, and listening skills, from the more sales-specific drivers of manager performance. As it turns out, management fundamentals account for roughly one-fourth of sales manager success. These are the foundational skills that are necessary for success in *any* management job, irrespective of function. Yet interestingly, we also found that performance on these attributes does not fall along a spectrum but tends to be binary. Either you're reliable or you're not. You have integrity or you don't. And that in turn tells us that these are inherent traits you should be looking for in the people you hire, not skills you want to be developing in your staff over time.

Put another way, great reps don't necessarily make great managers. You can't just excel at sales to be a great sales manager, you've also got to excel at *management* as well. Yet that is exactly how most companies still source new frontline management talent. This approach to hiring is the root cause of many organizations' high manager failure rates. Not surprisingly, our analysis of manager performance indicates that a handful of managers (roughly 4 percent in our sample) fail on at least one of these management fundamentals. So one of the first

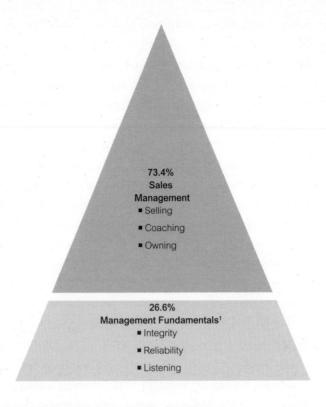

73.4%
Sales
Management
- Selling
- Coaching
- Owning

26.6%
Management Fundamentals[1]
- Integrity
- Reliability
- Listening

[1] Representative sample of management fundamental attributes.

Source: CEB, CEB Sales Leadership Council, 2011.

Figure 8.1. Management Fundamentals Are the Essential Base of Sales Manager Success

recommendations we make to our member companies completing the Sales Leadership Diagnostic is that they find new positions for managers who fall into this 4 percent. Because we haven't even gotten to the *sales-specific* attributes of a world-class manager, and these people have already failed to meet the manager bar.

On the other hand, while a star rep track record is not a reliable indicator of management potential, an alternative lies in the data presented in this chapter. Armed with an understanding of the star manager profile, organizations can adapt their candidate assessment protocols to look for candidates who are likely to demonstrate behaviors known to drive successful commercial outcomes. And knowing that some of these attributes are difficult (if not impossible) to develop over time—notably, management fundamentals like integrity and reliability—these are clearly places where it makes sense to screen up front.

However, traditional, interview-based assessment methods can be unreliable indicators of candidate potential and basic management ability. As a result, we find that progressive companies use a variety of experiential "live fire" assessment methods that let them see a candidate *do* the job before giving him the job. For example, one large high-tech manufacturer uses a full-day simulation-based skills assessment to precertify external candidates' management capabilities before employment offers are extended. A construction materials supplier uses a similar approach for internal candidates—its pre-promotion sales manager screening ensures that candidates possess and demonstrate the core combination of skills necessary to succeed as sales managers.

The Sales Side of Sales Manager Excellence

In the Army, there's an old saying that applies equally well to sales: "No plan survives engagement with the enemy." No matter how carefully one plans for battle, running through every possible scenario of what might happen and what might go wrong, the reality on the field will inevitably be different.

As a result, Army leaders have adopted a style of leadership known as Commander's Intent. Commander's Intent is just that: a clear, concise statement of the specific goal a commander is looking to achieve. Something like, "Capture and hold that hill until reinforcements arrive." In this approach to leadership, Army leaders have stopped giving step-by-step instructions on how to actually go about capturing the hill, because they've learned that once their troops get out in the field and engage in battle, they're going to have to quickly adapt to the situation on the ground in unanticipated ways.

Not surprisingly, then, the field leaders who excel in the Army are the ones who are creative, innovative, and able to adapt to their circumstances. Typically, they're the ones who recognize possible courses of action that no one behind the front would have recognized in advance and then guide their troops to victory through creative interpretation of their commander's intent. It's proven to be a powerful management philosophy that matches process on the one hand with empowerment and innovation on the other. When victory is on the line, put the battle in the hands of your best field-based leaders—the ones who identify a wide range of choices and develop an innovative option that specifically matches that particular situation.

As it turns out, when we studied the sales side of management excellence, the attributes that account for the remaining three-quarters of a sales manager's success, we found the same thing to be true. Figure 8.2 shows the sales attributes that matter most for manager excellence. Here is where our story shifts from preventing failure to promoting success.

When we ran the analysis, we found that the attributes contributing to manager excellence fall into three high-level categories—and they're about what you might expect: selling, coaching, and owning. This last category is all about the various aspects of business ownership that senior leaders like to see in managers—the extent to which they run their territory as if it were their own business.

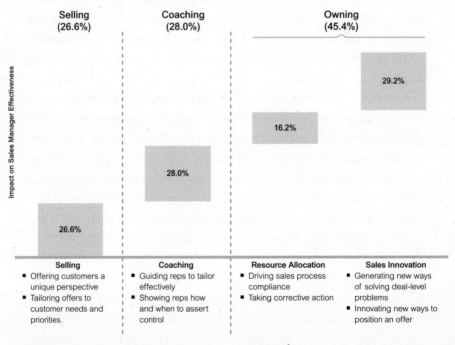

Note: Management fundamentals account for 26.6% of manager effectiveness, and sales management—selling, coaching, owning—accounts for the remaining 73.4%.
Source: CEB, CEB Sales Leadership Council, 2011.

Figure 8.2. Attributes Affecting Frontline Sales Manager Performance

Figure 8.2 represents the statistically significant factors that define the sales side of sales manager excellence (recalibrated to 100 percent, as they represent 100 percent of the sales side of the job). The first thing we can say about this side of the manager job is that selling still matters. To be sure, these results aren't saying that your best managers spend 25 percent of their time selling, but they do indicate that if we were to explain what makes your best managers so much better than everyone else, roughly 25 percent of the reason would be because of their great selling skills.

As all sales leaders know, selling skills are necessary at times since managers are often asked to cover vacant sales territories, to help close the largest sales, or just to fill in for a rep who may be on leave. But more to the point, managers are also expected to be able to model great selling behaviors for their teams.

What's especially interesting about the "Selling" bar on this chart, however, is the specific attributes that rose to the top inside that category. Here, we see that the same skills that matter most for manager success are the exact *same* sales skills we found to matter most for rep success: "Offers the customer unique perspectives," "Tailors the offer to the needs of customers," "Is comfortable discussing money." This implies that your best managers are likely going to come from your Challenger ranks, and it helps explain why top-performing managers are heavily sought after for the support they can provide on the largest, most complex deals—deals where Challenger skills, as we have seen, are most needed.

This brings us to the second driver, coaching, which accounts for 28 percent of frontline sales manager effectiveness. The size of this impact tells you what you probably expect: Coaching absolutely matters when it comes to sales management. It is a key element of manager effectiveness and, as we have long advocated to our members, a huge driver of rep performance as well.

Unlike selling, however, which is about a manager's ability to *be* a rep when needed, coaching is about the manager working side by side with reps to share his knowledge, insight, and experience to diagnose and correct specific rep behaviors known to hinder high performance.

When we look at the specific attributes of effective coaching, we find that the focus of these coaching efforts, at least for world-class managers, is again the same Challenger skills we saw in the selling category: "Guiding reps to tailor effectively," "Showing reps how and when to assert control," "Helping reps through complex negotiations." Coaching is such an important part of the manager effectiveness story that we'll spend a good portion of this chapter discussing it.

That said, it's not the whole story. While many sales leaders have come to simply equate good management with good coaching, it turns out that manager excellence is a matter of providing not *just* coaching but leadership, direction, and guidance more generally. It's about demonstrating effective ownership of the business. Indeed, our analysis shows that more than 45 percent of sales manager excellence is a function of excelling at managing the overall business. While great sales managers are fantastic at coaching their reps, they're even better at building their business. Great coaching is important, but it's still only part of the story.

Yet if we were to have guessed, we would have said that being an effective sales leader is mostly about how one allocates resources—things like driving process compliance, correcting actions out of step with that process, and managing resources across the territory as efficiently as possible. But it turns out that's not the case. All of these skills are captured in the resource allocation category—which at just over 16 percent is the smallest bar on the chart. What that tells us is that resource allocation isn't the most important part of a sales manager's job. In fact, it's the *least important* part of the manager's job.

So if "sales leadership" isn't about resource allocation, what *is* it about? Well, it turns out that sales leadership is mostly about how innovative sales managers are.

Now "innovation" is admittedly a loaded term that can mean many things to many people. What we're referring to here is managers collaborating with reps to understand as deeply as possible what's holding up a deal, figuring out why and where a deal is running into trouble at the customer, and then finding innovative ways to move it forward. It's important that innovation in this context is emphatically *not* about creating a new value proposition or inventing a new set of capabilities or product features. This is about creatively connecting the supplier's *existing* capabilities to each customer's unique environment and then presenting those capabilities to the customer through the specific lens of whatever customer obstacle is keeping that deal from closing.

This is Commander's Intent applied to the world of sales. It is about creatively modifying deal-level sales strategy to adapt to the specific customer context—the "reality on the ground," as it were. What this "Sales Innovation" factor tells us is that star-performing managers have an uncanny ability to unstick stuck deals and get them closed.

Notice how different this is from coaching. Coaching is about driving performance around known behaviors. It's a perfect approach to sales management in a world characterized by a predictable path to success. Innovation, on the other hand, is about driving performance through unforeseen obstacles. It's best suited to a world of dynamic and unexpected events. In coaching, the manager already knows the answer and imparts it to the rep. In innovation, neither the rep nor the manager knows the answer, so instead they collaborate through the manager's leadership to discover an effective path forward. You can't coach what you don't know, but you *can* innovate.

Arguably the biggest finding from all of our work on sales managers is just how important this skill really is. At 29 percent, sales innovation is the single biggest sales-related attribute contributing to world-class sales manager performance—more important than selling skills and much more important than a manager's ability to allocate resources.

While coaching is a close second at 28 percent, what's so interesting about sales innovation is that, unlike sales coaching, which has received a *huge* amount of time and attention over the last five years, it isn't something that most sales leaders have ever really thought about in any systematic fashion before.

If given a blank sheet of paper and asked to list the four to five attributes that account for manager success, how many of us, unprompted, would have included anything other than selling, coaching, and resource allocation on that list? And yet the data tells us that sales innovation is a distinctly important set of attributes. In their survey responses, reps often ranked a manager high on coaching attributes but low on sales innovation attributes, or vice versa. The two skills moved independently of one another.

Sales innovation is the missing link in terms of fully realizing the benefits of the Challenger Selling Model. Even armed with the best teaching pitches and honed capabilities for tailoring and taking control—even with strong sales managers who coach to these behaviors and can model the Challenger selling behaviors themselves—many deals will still not happen. While the Challenger model increases the likelihood that deals will move through the funnel, beating the status quo is a hard task. Customers are reluctant to change. The requirements for consensus continue to expand. Decision makers will continue to choose "no decision" even over a *good* decision. This is where the innovative manager comes in. Armed with the ability to innovate at the deal level, the manager can help the rep to avoid "no-decision land" more often than the rep—even a Challenger rep—can on her own. It's a critical capability in the battle to sell increasingly complex solutions to understandably ever more reluctant customers.

For most sales leaders on a mission to improve the effectiveness of their frontline sales managers, these data reveal a huge untapped opportunity to dramatically improve sales manager performance. Because of that, we're going to spend some time in this chapter digging into this concept of sales innovation to understand what it is, how it works, and, most important, how we can build it more systematically into our entire sales manager population.

Before we get into this notion of sales innovation in more detail, however, it first makes sense to engage in a deeper discussion around sales coaching. Formalized sales coaching represents one of the biggest opportunities to improve rep performance in a complex sales environment, but it is also one of the most misunderstood and mismanaged productivity levers.

COACHING TO THE KNOWN

To understand why coaching is often mismanaged by sales organizations, we need to start with a definition of coaching.

This is the definition of coaching that we've established with the help of a working team of members: "An ongoing and dynamic series of job-embedded interactions between a sales manager and direct report, designed to diagnose, correct, and reinforce behaviors specific to that individual." This definition lays out the foundation of coaching, and also how it differs from training.

There are a few points we always emphasize with our members in terms of this definition. First, coaching is *ongoing*—it's continuous as opposed to a one-off event or series of training events. Second, it involves diagnosis specific to the individual rep—so coaching is *customized*. Whereas training typically involves a one-size-fits-all approach of delivering the same teaching in the same format to everyone, coaching is completely tailored to an individual rep's specific needs. And finally, coaching is *behavioral*—it's not just about obtaining skill and knowledge; it's about demonstrated application of that skill and knowledge.

None of this is to suggest that training has no value. Training is good for sharing knowledge. Coaching is about acting upon it. The unique advantages of coaching stem from how it's tailored to the individual and systematically delivered at the point of need. Many organizations define coaching simply as "informal training," but our research has shown that effective coaching is, in fact, very formal. It's highly structured and regularly scheduled.

In the conversations we have with our members on this topic, there is another important distinction we make, which is how coaching differs from *managing*. While most frontline managers we speak with maintain that they do coach, for many, those efforts amount to little more than managing. We "tell" rather than "ask," we "do" rather than "guide."

The Business Case for Sales Coaching

Figure 8.3 (page 152)—which is one of the findings we are best known for—shows the huge impact that effective coaching can have on a sales organization.

When you improve coaching quality, the performance curve doesn't shift, it *tips*. The middle moves, but the feet don't. What exactly does that imply? First, moving from below-average to above-average coaching

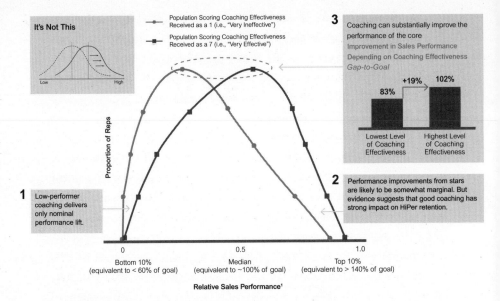

Figure 8.3. Distribution of Relative Sales Rep Performance by Coaching Effectiveness

appears to have little impact on our weakest performers, which seems counterintuitive. You'd imagine that these reps would be the easiest people to get a performance pop from if you just coached them a little better. But the bottom left of that chart tells us just the opposite. You can't coach away a bad fit for a job.

Likewise, the shift from weak to strong coaching doesn't have much of an impact on star performers either. This finding is also a bit counterintuitive, since you'd like to think that coaching could make stars even more stellar. The analogy we use is a professional golfer. Many of them have swing coaches and they work with them all the time. But in the end, they are hoping to shave *maybe* a stroke off their average. They're already high performers; they are only looking for slight, incremental improvements beyond their current level of play.

But if you're a core performer, the quality of the coaching you receive has a significant impact on your performance. The data from our research suggests that the median performers on your sales force could see a performance boost of as much as 19 percent given a significant improvement in the coaching they receive. The impact of simply moving from the bottom third to the top third of coaching effectiveness would still result in a performance gain of between 6 and 8 percent for the core of the sales force. Not many investments can deliver that sort of productivity lift to a sales organization.

This isn't just theoretical impact; it's real. We've seen this from the majority of the organizations we work with that have embarked on this coaching journey. One of our members, a major player in the insurance industry, saw a result similar to what our data suggests: a 10 percent improvement in rep performance for those reps who participated in the company's new coaching program versus those who didn't.

Coaching matters. Formalized coaching represents a huge performance improvement opportunity in a complex sales environment. It can make the difference between hitting or missing goal for the bulk of your sales force. Our strong recommendation to our members looking to improve sales performance is to do away with coaching democratically— that is to say, coaching everyone equally—and instead shift the majority of their coaching focus away from low and star performers and toward the core.

What's more, it turns out that coaching isn't just a huge driver of sales performance—it's also a major factor in employee retention and what we call "discretionary," or extra, effort. This was one of the bombshell findings from our original quantitative study on this topic, as it showed just how much impact coaching quality can have on employee morale. What the data tells us is this: Good coaches make people want to stay. Bad coaches, on the other hand, create a fundamentally demoralizing environment and drive people from the organization. This is true not just for our low performers but also for our core and star performers.

To corroborate this finding, we also cut the data by discretionary effort. We included a question in our survey that asked just how much effort people put into their working day in sales. Essentially, what we found is that bad coaching and bad managers make people want to give up. From low-performing reps to our superstars, none of them can be bothered if they don't feel they're getting effective coaching from their managers. Coaching quality matters.

Give Sales Managers Something to Coach To

When it comes to delivering quality coaching, the key lesson we've learned from several years of researching this topic is that managers can't coach effectively unless they have something to coach *to*. You can't just say, "Go forth and coach." You have to make it concrete for your managers. They need to have something to coach to: a clear understanding of what "good" looks like in your organization when it comes to sales (i.e., a hypothesis).

While we've documented a whole range of coaching best practices, tools, and templates, one of the smartest tactics we've seen employed for boosting sales coaching quality came to us from one of our members in the financial services industry. They built their new coaching process directly on top of their existing sales process, so that managers' coaching efforts are directly embedded into the sales activities they're already pursuing with their sales team.

In figure 8.4, you see a genericized version of what this company built for their sales managers. Each sales process stage has a different set of objectives. These are the behaviors critical to that stage that the company wants to reinforce. The tool also offers a number of sample questions a manager might ask to engage his reps in a coaching conversation around the objectives of that particular stage.

If you look at the first stage, "Opportunity Creation," as an example, the manager can consult this chart to verify the specific objectives and activities associated with this stage in the sales process. Things like setting and confirming a clear objective for the sales call, and completing sufficient pre-call research—things your high performers are probably already doing. Then, below that, you see the questions the manager can use to elicit how the rep is pursuing those objectives: for example, "What is your primary objective for this call?"

We've found that what often happens is that managers focus on outcomes rather than behaviors in coaching conversations, saying things like, "Your conversion rate is way down. What's the problem? Aren't you following the process?" That's not really what you should be after. Some members like to call that "spreadsheet coaching." It's focused on business results, not behaviors, and it's delivered in a

Where You Should Overweight Your Coaching Time Based on Demonstrated Best Practices

Sales Process Stage	Opportunity Creation	Opportunity Pursuit	Opportunity Closing	Ongoing Activities
Sample Stage-Aligned Coaching Objectives	▪ Verify client represents a valid opportunity and is a good fit for what we sell. ▪ Ensure rep conducts research to identify appropriate contacts within prospect/customer organization. ▪ Confirm rep has conducted sufficient pre-call planning and has a call or visit strategy specific to the institution.	▪ Ensure rep uses open-ended questions to identify and validate customer needs. ▪ Confirm rep uses an appropriate specialist in needs assessment and solutions development. ▪ Confirm proposed solutions link to verified needs. ▪ Ensure rep identifies potential deal blockers for the client and confronts barriers effectively.	▪ Confirm rep establishes priorities and deadlines with customer. ▪ Verify that rep determines the "correct" price to offer the customer. ▪ Ensure effective negotiation process occurs. ▪ Confirm the rep ensures customer's understanding of business plan.	▪ Verify that rep gathers post-deal customer feedback. ▪ Evaluate rep's coordination of deal across internal silos (e.g., divisions, functions, regions). ▪ Confirm rep establishes priorities and deadlines with customer.
Sample Stage-Aligned Coaching Starter Questions	▪ Let's role-play where I'm the client; show me what your first steps are in the call and how you'll earn my trust. ▪ What is your primary objective for this call? ▪ What did you do to prepare for the call today? ▪ Are there any signs you're looking for to know if this customer isn't a good fit? ▪ Share with me the three most important strategic initiatives of the client's institution.	▪ What questions do you think you will be asked? ▪ What will you look for to confirm this client is worth pursuing further? ▪ As you look through your solutions, have you asked "So what?" for this customer—what are the "so what's"? ▪ What do you think enabled you to have a two-way discussion with the customer? ▪ Do you feel you uncovered underlying needs?	▪ What barriers might you expect to encounter? ▪ Do you have a plan for repositioning the most at-risk elements of the deal? ▪ What do you think the nonmonetary business needs are in this negotiation? ▪ What is the toughest question they could ask you? How would you answer it? ▪ What internal resources might you use to close this deal?	▪ How do you plan to set a foundation for an ongoing relationship? ▪ Whom do you need to influence internally to make sure this deal succeeds? ▪ How do you plan to extricate yourself from this deal to focus on the next big opportunity? ▪ What are your next steps coming off that call?

Source: CEB, CEB Sales Leadership Council, 2011.

Figure 8.4. Sales Process–Aligned Coaching Guide

one-size-fits-all manner—everybody gets the exact same treatment. But done well, coaching is about behaviors, not outcomes. And that's exactly what makes this tool so effective. Even better, all of this is captured on a one-page road map that is really not much more complicated than what you see here. In fact, this company's sales managers carry laminated versions of this page with them in their bags.

This is the perfect cheat sheet to jump-start coaching conversations—without requiring a bunch of procedural hoops, training, and admin. In a world where most managers are, at best, skeptical about coaching, a tool like this goes a long way by giving managers a practical, nonintrusive framework for coaching that isn't overengineered and that doesn't require them to dramatically change their behavior.

In appendix A, we've provided an excerpt of our manager coaching guide built specifically to help reinforce the Challenger Selling Model (you can download the full version at our Web site). This is the same tool our Solutions group uses in its Challenger Development Program. Like the aforementioned sales process–aligned coaching guide on page 155, it maps to the pillars of the model—teaching, tailoring, and taking control—providing managers with guidance around what "good" looks like for each of these critical behaviors, as well as starter questions to facilitate coaching discussions.

Help Managers to "PAUSE" for Effective Coaching

The importance of the manager—and, specifically, the manager's role as coach—in making the Challenger model stick is almost impossible to overstate. Given the importance of good coaching to driving behavior change of this sort, we tell our members to start from the assumption that their coaching program is probably not working as well as it should be.

At CEB, we've worked with dozens of companies to help their sales managers improve their coaching abilities, teach deal innovation skills, and otherwise raise the quality of the frontline manager corps. One of the key components of our Manager Development Program is "Hypothesis-Based Coaching," which we think addresses the most pervasive issue companies struggle with when it comes to coaching: getting managers to execute the "double jump," from product-selling rep to solution-selling manager, becoming experts in observing sales interactions as well as experts in coaching based on those interactions. Hence, Hypothesis-Based Coaching, where managers enter coaching conversations with a clear hypothesis of what "good" looks like.

Hypothesis-Based Coaching leverages a powerful framework called "PAUSE," and it's something we encourage all of our members to use with their managers. Here's what PAUSE stands for:

- *Preparation for the Coaching Conversation:* Managers need to do proper and thorough preparation in advance of any coaching session. This provides continuity between coaching events. And by thinking through which stage of the sales process the rep is in, managers can tell what behaviors are going to be critical, which is the first step to solving the observation problem of situational variation.

- *Affirm the Relationship:* If the rep isn't ready to hear the coaching and buy into the manager's role as coach, the coaching effort will be wasted. Managers need to be taught how to emphasize development by separating performance management from coaching interactions—there is always a gray line, but it is possible to create "safe" situations for coaching to occur.

- *Understand Expected (Observed) Behavior:* The challenge for many managers is understanding what they are seeing and what to look for when observing their reps. If managers understand what should be happening in a meeting, it's much easier to know if it is happening.

- *Specify Behavior Change:* If managers know what defines critical behaviors and have an objective standard for judging those behaviors, it's very easy for them to provide specific objective feedback. This prevents coaching from being generic, subjective, ill focused, or overwhelming.

- *Embed New Behaviors:* The purpose here is to move a coaching program away from being all about the coaching moment and instead make it an institutionalized process. Companies should provide tools that allow managers to create action plans for each of their reps, give continuity to managers' coaching conversations, and give second-line sales managers a quantitative and qualitative view into their managers' coaching activities and abilities.

Again, we like this framework because it surmounts some of the big obstacles to delivering coaching effectively. We also find that the notion of PAUSE can be powerful for the manager because it suggests this idea of slowing down and thinking through the intent and purpose of the coaching interaction as opposed to making it a "check the box" activity as most time-pressed sales managers are naturally inclined to do. This approach helps ensure that one coaching conversation is a continuation of the last. It helps managers to keep coaching objective and prescriptive as it focuses on documented development opportunities. Getting coaching right is hard work, but ignoring it is *far* more painful—especially for an organization trying to install an ambitious change like the Challenger Selling Model—than taking the time to make sure it's properly designed and executed.

We've spent a fair amount of time talking about coaching because it absolutely is a pillar of world-class sales management. However, if we go back to the results of our analysis of manager effectiveness from earlier in this chapter, one of the surprises to our members is often that the coaching bar isn't actually *bigger*. Before we released these results, many of our members speculated that a good 50 percent or more of manager excellence would be attributable to whether they provide that coaching effectively.

That's not the case. It's fundamentally important, of course, but while coaching is certainly crucial for rep excellence, we now know that there's much more to the story of manager excellence. Let's take a look at the last element of manager effectiveness, sales innovation.

INNOVATING AROUND THE UNKNOWN

If sales innovation is the manager attribute that matters most, what does that mean sales managers should actually do in order to innovate?

Figure 8.5 shows the nine attributes that rose to the top as most important in defining the sales innovation factor. As you can see, these attributes sum into three key sales innovation activities: investigate, create, and share.

Investigating is all about the manager's ability to determine what exactly is getting in the way of advancing a sale. Who's involved? What decision criteria will they consider? What kind of financial concerns might get in our way? The innovative manager works closely with reps to map out, in as much detail as possible, the customer's decision-making process for any given deal—particularly one that's stalled somewhere along the line.

This is important, not just because most suppliers have only minimal information on how their customers make decisions, but because your

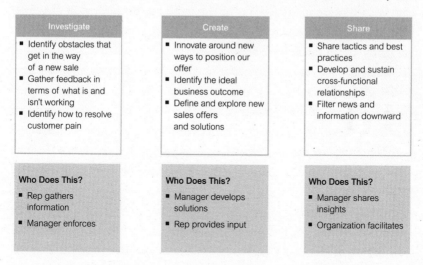

Investigate	Create	Share
■ Identify obstacles that get in the way of a new sale ■ Gather feedback in terms of what is and isn't working ■ Identify how to resolve customer pain	■ Innovate around new ways to position our offer ■ Identify the ideal business outcome ■ Define and explore new sales offers and solutions	■ Share tactics and best practices ■ Develop and sustain cross-functional relationships ■ Filter news and information downward
Who Does This? ■ Rep gathers information ■ Manager enforces	**Who Does This?** ■ Manager develops solutions ■ Rep provides input	**Who Does This?** ■ Manager shares insights ■ Organization facilitates

Source: CEB, CEB Sales Leadership Council, 2011.

Figure 8.5. Components of Sales Innovation

customers often aren't sure themselves how their organization makes decisions. Add to that your own efforts to sell more complex solutions to both new and existing customers and you're left facing an infinitely complex array of possible deal-level obstacles. This is the battlefield where the innovative manager really thrives: collaborating with reps to creatively identify where a specific deal is bogged down and then determining how to shake it loose.

The second way innovative managers stand out is by creating solutions. We are not suggesting that you should empower frontline sales managers to cobble together new solutions or invent new services. Remember, this isn't product innovation, it's sales innovation. But that still leaves innovative managers significant latitude to innovate at the deal level. This might include repositioning the supplier's capabilities to better connect to the customer's challenges or shifting risk from the customer to the supplier in exchange for a longer-term contract or access to additional cross-sale opportunities.

All of your managers spend a lot of time with reps working on deals, but most of that time is probably spent checking in on their work: "Did you call them back?" "Did you send the proposal?" "Did you mention the optional service package?" That's not solution creation, it's deal inspection, and we'd venture to say it takes up a good 70 to 80 percent of the time your managers spend with their reps. By contrast, innovation isn't about checking up on the rep. It's about co-creation (i.e., thought partnership) without value judgment, about working together collaboratively to find a better way to advance a deal. At the end of the day, you'll want your managers focusing their innovation efforts on those deals where the stakes are the highest—in other words, where their innovation time and effort is likely to pay the biggest returns. And if you think about it, we all have a few truly innovative managers. They're the ones who always find a way to get a deal done—even the ones that looked as though they had no chance at all of making it. And it's the solutions they come up with that often become the stuff of interoffice legend across the sales team. "Did you hear how Bob managed to help Cindy close the Smith account?" "Yeah, that was brilliant! How does he come up with this stuff?" One of our members called these managers "sales ninjas." It's a funny term, but when you think about it, it kind of fits. These people are masters of every tool of the trade. They can find a way in when no one else can.

Finally, innovative managers eagerly and actively share the fruit of their innovation efforts. There's huge value in being able to replicate the application of that innovation elsewhere if you can just capture it in ways that others can learn from. This is how you get scale from all those innovation efforts. Innovative managers are all about sharing best practices, developing and sustaining a strong relationship network inside the organization, and passing new ideas and solutions to the rest of the team.

So now that we've got a better sense of what sales innovation is all about, let's go back and compare it with the other part of the ownership category of manager excellence. There are some really important implications we will discuss regarding how well resource allocation and sales innovation can peacefully coexist.

Worlds in Conflict

When we discussed the "portrait of a world-class sales manager" earlier in this chapter, you'll recall that the required profile of the sales manager has really changed to become more of a *leadership* profile. World-class managers today are defined not just by their ability to coach to the *known*, but by their ability to innovate around the *unknown*.

This is critically important for an organization pursuing the Challenger model. Even with Challengers armed with effective teaching pitches and the right skills to tailor and take control of the sale, overcoming the customer's status quo is not going to happen 100 percent of the time. Many deals will still go off the rails and get bogged down. Here's where an innovative manager can make all the difference between closing a deal and chalking up another loss to "no decision."

Unfortunately, you'll also recall that when it comes to boosting manager effectiveness, most sales leaders tend to place their biggest bet on *resource allocation*—that is, directing frontline sales managers to more efficiently manage their limited resources through better territory management, deal qualification, and sales process compliance. When you think about it, that's what resource allocation is all about: efficiency. Sales innovation, on the other hand, is very much about effectiveness.

Yet as figure 8.6 (page 162) shows, when you look at the impact of an efficiency focus on manager performance compared with an effectiveness focus, you find that an effectiveness focus has nearly twice the impact of an efficiency approach.

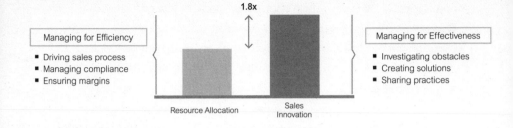

Source: CEB, CEB Sales Leadership Council, 2011.

Figure 8.6. The Relative Impact of Resource Allocation and Sales Innovation on Manager Effectiveness

Now, just to be clear, we would never say that driving process efficiency is wrong for a sales organization. But efficiency is all about doing what you *already know how to do* better and better. Let's get the right reps chasing the right customers, engaged in the right activities. And let's do that again and again and again. If possible, faster each time.

But that kind of single-track focus on efficiency only works if every deal is the same. If you live in a world of knowable needs, findable business, and predictable customer behavior, then lock down process and coach the heck out of it. For most sales managers, that's a pretty accurate description of their worlds five or six years ago, when straightforward product selling was still a relatively large part of their business. But that's not the world most sales leaders are living in today. If they're going to grow revenue in today's environment, driving efficiency around the *known* must give way—in part at least—to an ability to collaboratively innovate around the *unknown*. As one member told us, "If we had religiously followed our sales process last year, our three biggest deals would have never gotten done."

Sales success today is much less about getting better at what you already know and much more about creating an ability to tackle what you *don't know*. In order to thrive in that world, you're going to have to build a sales organization—and a sales culture—that enables that kind of innovation activity. A world where effectiveness is elevated above efficiency. However, we find that most sales organizations have a long way to go on that front—look at figure 8.7.

Source: CEB, CEB Sales Leadership Council, 2011.

Figure 8.7. Sales Manager Response to Question "Do you think that senior management at your company is more or less likely to encourage and support the following?"

In a recent survey of frontline sales managers, we asked respondents how they would characterize the current strategy of their senior leadership team based on a range of attributes and behaviors. And the answer was very clear. Most managers told us they currently operate in an environment dominated by a strong emphasis on efficient execution of the sales process. Meanwhile, almost *no* managers agreed with the statement that "leadership empowers managers to set their own course of action." Yet in that same survey, managers also told us that they believe that empowerment—or freedom to make decisions—is in fact the *most important* factor in their current success. And our own study of sales manager effectiveness would suggest they're right.

Now, to be sure, every organization has to have enforceable rules. Certainly, we need to set targets around specific business outcomes and push to attain them. But within that context, we still need to find a way to empower managers to pursue those ends with innovative means. Yet few companies appear to have the kind of culture in place to allow that to happen. This is the rather sobering message of this seemingly innocuous finding: At a time when sales leaders need to "get back to growth," the growth engine for most organizations is built atop the wrong chassis. Your organization is designed for efficiency at a time when effectiveness is going to win the day. What the data suggests is that most organizations have a long way to go to build a culture where sales innovation can thrive.

While shifting from an efficiency- to an effectiveness-focused sales culture is a long-term migration for any company, the good news is that there are certainly things that you can do right away to help equip your sales managers to be more innovative at the deal level.

Helping Managers to Understand Their Biases

As it turns out, the kind of thinking managers rely on every day to do many other aspects of their job well is one of the biggest obstacles to their being innovative. In figure 8.8, you see that we call this kind of thinking "narrowing thinking." Narrowing thinking is all about looking at a complex problem, weighing existing options, and producing a single solution. It's incredibly valuable in a world where managers must make tough, rapid decisions on things like allocating scarce resources. Unfortunately, at the same time, narrowing thinking also severely limits managers' ability to develop creative solutions to hard-to-solve customer challenges, as it's focused on eliminating options from consideration rather than generating new ones for consideration.

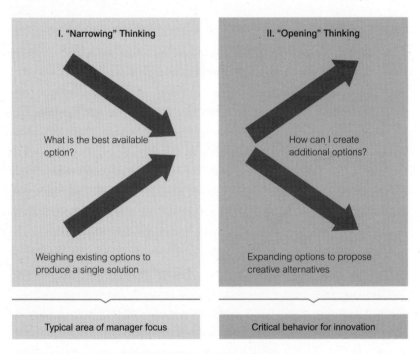

I. "Narrowing" Thinking

What is the best available option?

Weighing existing options to produce a single solution

Typical area of manager focus

II. "Opening" Thinking

How can I create additional options?

Expanding options to propose creative alternatives

Critical behavior for innovation

Source: Morgan D. Jones, "The Thinker's Toolkit"; CEB, CEB Sales Leadership Council, 2011.

Figure 8.8. Modes of Manager Thought

The alternative is "opening thinking," which is characterized by the generation and vetting of as many alternative options as possible. While narrowing thinking may be better for resource management, opening thinking is better for deal innovation. If you're going to build innovative managers, you'll have to overcome managers' natural inclination—and day-to-day pressure—to think narrowly, and equip them with tools and frameworks to think openly, at least at those times when sales innovation is called for. To do that well, the first thing an organization needs to do is to effectively raise their awareness of what's getting in the way of opening thinking in the first place.

Decades of research into human behavior has uncovered a number of human biases that commonly hinder opening thinking. The six most common are:

- Practicality bias: Ideas that seem unrealistic should be discarded.
- Confirmation bias: Unexplainable customer behaviors can be ignored.
- Exportability bias: If it didn't work here, it won't work anywhere.
- Legacy bias: The way we've always done it must be best.
- First conclusion bias: The first explanation offered is usually the best or only choice.
- Personal bias: If I wouldn't buy it, the customer won't either.

These biases are not inherently "bad." In fact, these are mental tools we all use every day to help us rapidly sort through large amounts of information and make decisions more quickly. These are basically filters that allow all of us—and especially time-strapped sales managers—to make rapid decisions in the face of complexity. This ability is critically important to their success.

At the same time, however, each of these biases effectively cuts off certain paths of inquiry. They help us to make decisions quickly, but at the sacrifice of making decisions thoroughly, as each of these biases leads us to view the world exclusively from our own perspective. That can be deadly in the world of sales, as it means managers often fail to place themselves in the shoes of their customer, not because they're bad managers, but because they're human. They sit down with a rep, look at a deal that appears hopelessly stalled, and seeing the world through these biases, fail to uncover an innovative way to move that deal forward.

There are two simple means of helping managers overcome these biases and open up their thinking. The first is simply to make managers aware of these biases in the first place. Just informing managers that the biases exist—and reminding them on an ongoing basis—can significantly reduce their natural tendency to self-censor in this manner. Second, we can train managers to ask themselves (and their reps) specific questions to prompt thinking from alternate perspectives.

Let's dig into this idea of "prompting questions" in a little bit more detail to really understand how it works.

Holding Biases at Bay

Simply put, prompting questions are a forcing mechanism to expand your thinking. Good prompting questions encourage us to do one of three things when considering a problem or situation: deepen our understanding, broaden our perspective, or expand our ideas.

	1. Deepen Understanding	2. Broaden Perspectives	3. Expand Ideas
Purpose:	Helps managers overcome tendency to propose or discard solutions before gaining a complete understanding of the problem at hand.	Helps managers overcome tendency to understand challenges exclusively from a personal or sales-centric perspective.	Helps managers overcome tendency to consider only ideas that are consistent with existing assumptions about what is possible.
Examples:	▪ What is the bigger picture that this customer situation fits into? ▪ What else must be going on behind the scenes for this to be true?	▪ If you were the customer's CFO, what would you look for in this offering? ▪ What's the head of marketing going to think when he sees this proposal?	▪ What would you do differently if you had more budget to pursue this customer? ▪ What steps would you pursue if the timeline expanded from six months to one year?
When to Use:	Managers should use if they tend to default to a "one-size-fits-all" strategy regardless of the problem at hand.	Managers should use if they tend to overrely on personal experience for understanding, even when it is not relevant.	Managers should use if they tend to discard ideas in the name of practicality before allowing them to fully develop.

Source: CEB, CEB Sales Leadership Council, 2011.

Figure 8.9. Characteristics of Effective Prompting Questions

Many prompting questions are designed to help us fully explore our understanding of an issue before drawing conclusions. For instance, "What's the bigger picture that this customer situation falls into?" or "What else must be going on behind the scenes for this to be true?"

These types of questions are great for helping managers avoid defaulting too quickly to a one-size-fits-all answer.

Second, there are questions that force us to consider alternate viewpoints. Questions like, "If you were the customer's CFO, how would you view this offering?" or "What's the head of marketing going to think when he sees this proposal?" are especially useful questions for managers who tend to believe they've got all the answers already.

Finally, there are questions that encourage us to temporarily set aside practicality concerns that limit our thinking. A good question here might be, "What would you do differently if you had more budget to pursue this customer?" These are great questions for managers who run too quickly to all of the reasons why we *can't* do something, rather than explore how we *could* do something.

How could something like this work in practice with sales managers? Take a look at the tool in figure 8.10.

Challenge: *Customers are resistant to a price increase.*

Innovation	Description	Potential Ideas
Substitute	What could we potentially use in its place?	
Combine	How can we integrate, mix, or combine with other offerings?	*Bundle it with another product that the customer values.*
Adapt	What outside ideas could be adapted to our situation?	
Magnify	How can we add to or increase our emphasis on a valuable feature?	
Modify	How can we change attributes of the offer to make it more relevant?	*Sell them smaller quantities with greater frequency.*
Put to another use	How might a different function in the customer organization value this?	*Find a secondary use for our product in their manufacturing process*
Eliminate	What elements that customers are unwilling to pay for can be removed?	*Eliminate unnecessary packaging costs to offset price increase.*
Rearrange	How can we change the order of things to make them more relevant?	
Reverse	How can we reverse our approach to do the exact opposite?	

It is not necessary to answer all questions for the SCAMMPERR Framework to be effective.

Source: Michal Michalko, "Thinkertoys: A Handbook of Creative Thinking Techniques" (2006); CEB, CEB Sales Leadership Council, 2011.

Figure 8.10. SCAMMPERR Framework

We've pulled together an entire library of prompting question tools for our members, but this is one of our favorites and one that a number of our members have put to good use in their own sales organizations. It's called the "SCAMMPERR Framework"—the name comes from the first letter of each word down the first column—and it's a classic tool used to facilitate brainstorming exercises.

What's beautiful about this tool is how simple it is. It's a very straightforward way to equip your managers to systematically probe a deal for innovation potential without having to somehow rewire their brains or put them through years of training. As you read through this, notice that while the tool itself may be unfamiliar, you'll probably recognize much of this as exactly the kind of thing your star-performing managers do automatically almost every day.

Let's say that a manager is working with a rep to advance a deal that has become bogged down due to the customer's strong resistance to a price increase. Of course, you know how the rep would propose moving that deal forward. If price is the problem, then the price is too high. You should offer them a discount.

Rather than narrowing immediately to that solution, however, the innovative manager will use a tool like this to broaden their thinking on what to do next. Using the tool, a sales manager can articulate a series of ways in which this deal might be repositioned in order to make it more palatable to the customer without having to modify the price. Prompting questions like "What might we substitute?" or "How might we combine this offer with others?" or "What ideas that have worked elsewhere can be adapted to this situation?" force the manager and rep to think more expansively before running to offer a discount.

In keeping with the example, under "Modify," perhaps we can sell the customer smaller quantities with greater frequency. Or under "Eliminate," maybe we can get rid of unnecessary or customized packaging in order to offset price increases. It's not necessary to answer every question for the SCAMMPERR tool to work. The framework is simply a forcing mechanism to help managers expand the universe of possible actions. Again, this is one of the many innovation tools we've developed for our members.

BRINGING IT HOME

Now that we've discussed the important role of the frontline manager in this story, it's time to turn to some of the implementation lessons that we've learned from helping companies to build their own Challenger sales organizations.

9

IMPLEMENTATION LESSONS FROM THE EARLY ADOPTERS

Since unveiling the Challenger findings in 2009, CEB has been helping sales and marketing leaders to adopt the Challenger Selling Model in their own organizations. We've learned a lot from the experiences of these early adopters. This chapter provides implementation lessons for sales, marketing, and senior leaders informed by our experience in the field.

LESSONS FOR SALES LEADERS

Not Every High Performer Is a Challenger

It's easy for executives to slip into the trap of assuming that all their high performers are, by definition, Challengers. There are lots of things that all high performers do, but only some of them (roughly 40 percent, according to our data) get there by teaching, tailoring, and taking control.

Part of the Challenger Selling Model is institutionalizing what your Challengers do naturally—studying the way they teach, tailor, and take control within your specific industry, with your specific customers, and sharing that knowledge with your entire sales force. To do this effectively, you need to be sure you aren't mistakenly documenting the tactics and habits of a high-performing Relationship Builder or Lone Wolf.

It's absolutely critical that companies first correctly identify their Challengers before they can observe how their Challengers are selling to customers right now. Just asking managers to identify their Challengers won't work, as they're more likely to pick their high performers, regardless of actual selling style.

CEB uses a diagnostic for companies that is built off the original Challenger survey; it asks the same set of questions that we used to create the Challenger Selling Model. You can find a simplified version in appendix B to give you a sense of what that diagnostic looks like.

Just as every high performer is not necessarily a Challenger, not every Challenger is a high performer. We've found some organizations with "inactive" Challengers—they have the right skills but aren't aware of how to apply them. Once they are exposed to the framework of teaching, tailoring, and taking control, these skills become "activated" in a new and powerful way.

Beware the Call of the Lone Wolf

Close observers of our research could make the argument that Lone Wolves actually have the highest *probability* of being high performers—and, technically, they would be correct. While Lone Wolves represent the smallest percentage of the overall sample of sales reps (at 18 percent), a full 25 percent of all high performers fall into the Lone Wolf profile—in other words, of all the profiles, the chances are greatest that a Lone Wolf pulled out of a crowd would actually be a high performer. But jumping from this observation to the conclusion that all reps should be Lone Wolves is a folly.

An all–Lone Wolf sales force follows no pattern. By definition, Lone Wolves don't follow any process or set of rules aside from their own. That makes it impossible to model and replicate their behaviors across the sales organization. The top performers in this kind of environment may do well, but there's no way to bring your core performers up to their level in the same manner.

Lone Wolves also struggle in the collaborative, team-based environments required to bring more complex solutions to customers. As a VP of sales from a high-tech company recently told us, "In our organization, we are moving rapidly to having to sell as a *team* instead of selling individually. Lone Wolves are a cancer in an environment like this." While individual Lone Wolves can be effective on their own, a team of them is a team that doesn't sell anything.

We have also found that sales rep profiles are in part a function of their environment. Reps will generally pursue the approach that will make them the most money—whatever their company rewards and celebrates. If Lone Wolves dominate a sales organization, this is most likely because those reps are being told, explicitly or implicitly, to try to figure out what works on their own. In this kind of environment, the company loses all credibility and is seen by reps not as an authority on what customers value—a source of intelligent guidance and counsel—but as a roadblock to a rep's success. The company, in the Lone Wolf sales force, is an entity to be avoided because it adds no value to a salesperson. The things the company has developed, like training, sales process, CRM, tools, and many more, are of little value to the Lone Wolf. While reps may hit quota in an organization like this, it is in spite of, not because of, the support and guidance provided by management.

Start Recruiting for Challengers Yesterday

We believe strongly that Challengers can be built. As we roll out our Challenger training, we're finding that reps are *excited* to play this role with their customers, and once the model is unlocked for them, they can start challenging their customers right away. However, it also makes sense for companies to start recruiting Challengers to replace any reps who naturally turn over within the organization or to fill new positions made available as the organization grows.

Hiring for Challengers requires a different approach to interviewing and screening. We provide a Challenger Hiring Guide to help with the process (you can find it in appendix C). The guide is organized around the key competencies of the Challenger rep. It offers sample questions an interviewer might ask, stipulates what the evaluation standard should be for each competency, and then offers some red flags to look out for. For instance, one of the competencies of the Challenger is the ability to offer a unique perspective to the customer. An interviewer can probe for this by asking questions like, "How do you usually open a sales conversation with a customer?" or "Can you describe a time when you got a customer to think of their problem or need differently?" The interviewee's pitches should highlight customer benefits before supplier strengths and, ideally, offer unique insights that prompt the customer to think differently about their world. The key red flags to watch out for are feature- and benefit-focused pitches.

This tool has been successfully adopted by many of our members. One of the companies we work with in the beverage industry reports that their new reps, recruited using the Challenger guide, are "running circles around the existing sales team."

While we've also heard some success stories from members using commercially available prehire screening tools to identify Challengers, this has come mainly from retrofitting existing tools to "search for" Challengers out in the labor market. While there are many prehire assessment tools available for sales, none have been built specifically to identify Challengers. Until somebody offers a fix for this problem, we recommend that sales leaders use caution when leveraging existing prehire assessment tools to screen for a profile they weren't actually designed to identify.

Individual Skill and Organizational Ability Are Best Developed in Parallel

While it's clear that companies must invest in both organizational capabilities and individual skills to get the full benefit of the Challenger Selling Model, it's less clear whether there is a proper sequencing of those investments. Should companies first build organizational capabilities or develop rep skills? This is a question we hear often from our members. Our answer is that the best organizations will invest in both elements of the model concurrently.

We have heard from companies that attempted to develop Commercial Teaching messages without also boosting sales rep awareness and skills that their reps rejected the new teaching messages, preferring to go back to what they're comfortable and familiar with. Similarly, companies that invested in rep skills but not in organizational capabilities left reps feeling that they lacked the tools to truly execute on the model as it was intended to be employed. By contrast, organizations that pursue both tracks simultaneously are primed for effective, dynamic collaboration. Reps, seeing the power of the Challenger approach, create pull-through demand for teaching messages from marketing, while marketing, having similarly bought into the vision of the Challenger approach, enlists sales as a powerful source of insight raw materials (i.e., messages being delivered by high-performing Challengers right now).

Don't Just Change the Training, Change What Happens Before and After

Outside of compensation, sales training represents one of the biggest discretionary spending areas for a sales organization. It also represents one of the biggest time and money sinks. Research by Neil Rackham has shown that 87 percent of sales training content is forgotten by reps within thirty days.

The Challenger Selling Model requires large-scale behavior change from reps, putting heightened pressure on sales L&D (learning and development) functions to deliver change and sustain it over time. Coaching is a principal lever for boosting training stickiness. But there are other important considerations as well. In a recent study, we found that some of the biggest opportunities for improving sales training content retention have little to do with improving the training itself. Instead, it's what companies can do before and after training that really makes a difference.

Leading companies are doing three things to significantly boost the ROI of their training investments: First, they are boosting rep demand for change and generating training buzz before it is rolled out; second, they are engineering high-quality experiential learning that gives reps a sense of "safe practice" focused on real accounts; and third, they are creating sustained behavioral certification programs to reinforce learning over time.

This is one of the big differences in the way our Solutions group has designed our Challenger Development Program. While the content of the training is obviously unique since it is built around the Challenger behaviors, it's also about helping member companies generate the sort of "social demand" they need in order to avoid the perception that the training is just another top-down mandate. In addition, we focus heavily on the concept of "safe practice," delivering experiential learning in the classroom that's led by former sales leaders from companies like DuPont, Merck, Nike, IBM, Bank of New York Mellon, and Procter and Gamble. And it's important that we get beyond the usual "did you learn anything?" assessments that most companies focus on as a way to gauge whether training "stuck" at all with reps, and instead focus on a structured approach to reinforcing the training on an ongoing basis (spending a lot of time with managers, who will drive this change through ongoing coaching) so that we can certify that reps are actually *practicing* the new behaviors they learned in the classroom and achieving the intended sales results.

These principles are smart to adhere to. We advise all of our members to think hard about the "before and after" of their training so that they can make sure there's demand for it among reps and so that they know they're getting a return on this important investment.

LESSONS FOR MARKETING LEADERS

Stop Telling the World How "Customer-centric" You Are

More than ever before, suppliers are emphasizing how they put "the customer first." The assumption is that if you want to grow coming out of the recent downturn, you're going to have to ensure that everything you do delivers maximum customer value. But there are several ways to be "customer-centric" that are actually bad for business. Two examples of this that we hear frequently from our members are (1) discounts and other terms and conditions that undermine profitability in exchange for little long-term gain, and (2) assuming an order-taker posture with the customer (i.e., taking short-term orders when the customer is pushing for them, instead of getting them to think about longer-term business).

We have heard the term "customer-centricity" so overused that it has been completely watered down. Just because you involve customers in your R&D process, for example, does not mean your average sales rep understands, as one of our members put it, "what your key customer does and struggles with for ten hours a day in their office." That is customer-centricity in the sales world—and it's very rare that reps have this.

The bottom line is very simple: If you truly want to build a "customer-centric" organization, then you're actually going to have to build an *insight-centric* organization—a commercial enterprise specifically designed to generate new-to-the world insights that teach customers to think differently not about your products and solutions, but about their business.

There Is No Sidestepping the "Deb Oler Question"

"Why should your customers buy from you instead of your competitors?" If you can't answer this question, you don't have a Challenger Selling Model.

The Challenger approach is about reframing the customer's worldview, giving them a new way to think about how to save or make money. There are lots of ideas for saving and making money that your customers might value, but most of these aren't going to link back to capabilities where you outperform the competition. If you can't say what differentiates you—why your customers should buy from you instead of a competitor—you can't teach them to value what makes you different.

Every company has *some* unique differentiator, otherwise they probably wouldn't exist. That said, when it comes to the insights that lead to those unique benefits, there's no need to start from scratch. Savvy marketing organizations understand that they have Challengers out in the field right now teaching customers new insights that can jump-start their own efforts to build more scalable—and sustainable—Commercial Teaching capabilities.

Never Put These Ten Words in Your Pitch Deck

Take a close look at your standard pitch deck, the "about us" section on your corporate home page, or your PR material. Highlight every instance of the words "leading," "unique," "solution," or "innovative." In particular, go find all instances of the phrase "We work to understand our customers' unique needs and then build custom solutions to meet those needs." Then hit the delete key. Because every time you use one of those buzzwords, you are telling your customers, "We are exactly the same as everyone else."

Ironically, the more we try to play up our differences, the more things sound the same. Public relations expert Adam Sherk recently analyzed the terms used in company communications, and the results are devastating. Here are the top ten:

	BUZZWORD/MARKETING SPEAK/ OVERUSED TERM	MENTIONS IN PRESS RELEASES
1.	Leader	161,000
2.	Leading	44,900
3.	Best	43,000
4.	Top	32,500
5.	Unique	30,400
6.	Great	28,600
7.	Solution	22,600
8.	Largest	21,900
9.	Innovative	21,800
10.	Innovator	21,400

By definition, there can be only one leader in any industry—and 161,000 companies each think they're it. More than 75,000 companies think they're the "best" or the "top"; 30,400 think they're "unique." "Solution" also makes an appearance at number seven—so if you think that calling your offering a "solution" differentiates you, think again. If everyone's saying they offer the "leading solution," what's the customer to think? We can tell you what their response will be: "Great—give me 10 percent off."

In all of our time with members, we have never once met one who doesn't think her company's value proposition beats the socks off the competitors'. And it's understandable. After all, why would we want to work for a company whose product is second-rate—especially when our job is to sell that product? But what the utter sameness of language here tells us is that, ironically, a strategy of more precisely describing our products' advantages over the competition's is destined to have the exact opposite effect—we simply end up sounding like everyone else.

Our members' customers told us the same thing: As great as your products are, they're not *that* much different from the competition. No matter how much you tell customers, "We're here to create quantifiable business value," keep in mind that the next sales rep through the door is saying the exact same thing. We once spoke to a procurement executive at a food company who told us, "Every time I hear the word 'value,' my defenses go up, because that's when I know they're trying to sell me something." Just as a parent can tell twins apart in a way no one else can, you can see your products' nuances and their uniqueness—but your customers probably can't.

That said, it *is* possible to differentiate yourself from the competition. The trick is not to describe your differences, but to make customers value them. And to do that, remember these two things: First, be memorable, not agreeable. It's nice to have a business conversation about profits and capabilities, or a relationship conversation around sports and kids, but unless you frame your conversation around an edgy or unique insight, the customer will forget everything you said as soon as you walk out the door. Being different sounds risky, but it's better than being forgettable.

Second, build a pitch that leads *to* your solution, not *with* it. Before even talking about your capabilities, teach customers about a problem they didn't even know they had—one that you can solve better than your competitors. Only then should you lead into the details of your specific solution.

LESSONS FOR ALL SENIOR LEADERS

Tolerate (Limited) Rejection of the Model

One of the questions we get frequently is about high performers who aren't Challengers. Should organizations force reps who beat quota—but are more naturally disposed to a different, non-Challenger selling approach—to change how they engage with customers? Our answer is no, you shouldn't, but there are some important caveats here.

One of the lessons we've learned about any type of change in the sales organization is that companies shouldn't shoot for 100 percent adoption. We've found that the best companies shoot for 80 percent adoption of any change—whether a new skill, tool, process, or system. The final 20 percent is always hugely painful to attain. Exemplars shoot for 80 percent and let the rest of the organization come along at their own pace, provided these reps are beating goal (and not being detrimental to the broader transformation effort).

The same rule applies for driving the Challenger approach among sales reps. Some reps will simply buck the journey and point to their performance as evidence that they don't need to change. This is fine, but only as long as they continue to beat goal. The way we think about it is this: When a new standard for sales excellence has been defined by the organization (in this case, the Challenger Selling Model), those who refuse to make the journey are effectively the new Lone Wolves. And as we discussed earlier in this book, the rule of thumb for managing a Lone Wolf is "live by the sword, die by the sword." The minute their performance slips, they need to adopt the new approach or relinquish their seat in the organization to somebody else who will.

High performers share a common code—they are always eager to understand how they can improve their own performance. Therefore, they are usually the *first* reps to want to try something new. Think of these reps as your elite athletes. Athletic high performers are always looking for that extra edge. If there is a new technology that helps, they adopt it. If there's a new training approach they believe in, they incorporate it. If there is a new skill that's been shown to yield better results, they want it. High-performing salespeople are no different. They are the ones who will read up on sales (many of them have probably beaten you to the punch in reading this book). They are always on the lookout for messaging, tools, and ways to position deals that have been tried successfully by their peers.

But like elite athletes, high-performing reps are highly discriminating. If they don't see value in a new approach, they will reject it.

Therefore, if companies can identify their high-performer Challengers (as well as high-performer managers who exhibit Challenger skills) and turn them into champions early on, the rest of the organization is likely to follow.

Right now, the Challenger Selling Model is a novel approach, but soon it will become the standard. Those who refuse to adopt it will find it increasingly difficult to engage with customers when those very customers are being engaged by reps from other companies who *are* employing Challenger methods. The state of the art moves and evolves. Advantages accrue to the early adopters, to be sure, but eventually adoption isn't an option anymore; it's a requirement.

For sales leaders struggling with that "final 20 percent" who refuse to make the journey now, it's really just a matter of time. If these reps are beating quota, let them sell their way. But they'll find that overperformance harder to attain year after year, will get frustrated as others in the organization displace them on the President's Club rankings, and they'll give the new methods a shot too.

Expect Casualties

Some of your reps—in our experience, between 20 and 30 percent—probably won't make the transition to the Challenger model. Maybe they're just too stuck in their ways, or maybe when they see the Challenger profile, their reaction is, "Whoa, that's not what I signed up for."

This doesn't mean they're bad employees. But it also doesn't mean you'd want them in a quota-carrying role, especially on your more complex accounts. Many of our members have found these individuals to be extremely well suited, for example, to a customer service role, or perhaps even more intriguing, for a marketing or product specialist role—places where they know the frontline business well, but aren't on the hook to face off with customers in a challenging manner in the same way a sales rep will need to.

Either way, keep in mind that if 20 to 30 percent of your sales force *can't* make the transition, that means that 70 to 80 percent *can*. And that's really good news for sales leaders. Remember, this isn't about rewiring people's DNA or changing who they are as a person. It's about equipping them with the skills, tools, and coaching they need to *act* like a Challenger when they're in front of the customer—and that's something many reps not only are able to do, but also are excited to try. It offers them a whole new and much more concrete path to professional success than they've ever had in the past. We're not asking reps to change *who they are*, just how they sell.

Consider Piloting Before Broadly Launching

W. W. Grainger, Inc., profiled in chapter 5, took a very careful, pilot-based approach to rolling out their new sales model and teaching collateral. Most companies pilot new tools to understand what modifications should be made before launching them to the entire organization, but Grainger goes one step further. They pilot tools to understand when and why adoption will plateau. They're after four questions, specifically:

1. How big is the early adopter group for this tool (i.e., when is the adoption curve likely to plateau)?
2. Who are the early adopters, and how are they different from nonadopters?
3. What metrics can we track to more accurately predict the impact of this tool?
4. What can we learn from this experience to improve tool impact and push greater adoption among the majority who don't adopt?

By answering these questions, Grainger's sales operations team can build a plan for how to break through adoption plateaus when they occur.

Grainger finds that reps naturally cluster into one of the following time-based segments when deciding whether to adopt a tool: early adopters, majority, laggards, and naysayers. Pushing too early for adoption to a given segment before successfully winning over the previous segment can be a waste of organizational energy. For example, the majority population waits to observe early tool success, while the laggards need to see success from a peer closer to their segment before acceptance will occur. Targeting the correct population at the right time with the appropriate advocates and through the right channels is the key to driving adoption beyond the "chasm" that companies normally hit once the early adopters have all adopted—very similar to rolling out a new product to the market.

One additional note about the Grainger adoption practice: Proximity matters. Something sales managers love to do is to tell their average performers to do what their high performers do. But modeling star-performing sales behavior as a way of "selling" change internally can actually lead to failure. In terms of prescribing the right actions, following high-performer behavior is the right play—and this book goes into some detail about our perspective on a specific set of high-performer behaviors that you should replicate—but when it comes time to roll this change out, this approach of "do what the high performers are doing" can actually do more harm than good.

Why? People don't start using tools or practicing certain behaviors because star performers have success—they use them because people *just like them* are having success. To roll this new approach out to the broader sales force, you also need to look for and document examples of *average performers* in different markets or with different product portfolios who went from non-Challenger to Challenger and had success doing it. And that obviously can't happen without the right type of pilot.

Terminology Matters

We know that the term "Challenger" can rub people the wrong way. We've heard every manner of pushback here you can imagine. Some companies fear it will make their reps think it's okay to be aggressive or brutish in the market. Others fear that drawing a contrast with the Relationship Builder will make reps think that relationships are no longer important to your business.

Some of our members have asked us why we wouldn't instead call the Challenger the "New Relationship Builder" if, in fact, we are saying that the Challenger actually builds *stronger* relationships with customers. The reason is simple: Nobody cares about "New Relationship Builders." In case you don't believe us, ask yourself this: Would you have bought this book if it was about how to build "New Relationship Builders"? The answer is almost certainly no.

In order to get the organization to pay attention to the change you are driving, you must create cognitive dissonance. There must be a moment when reps understand, very clearly, to "do this, not that." If the new model feels like a tweak on the old . . . well, why bother changing? Change, after all, is hard work. If reps see a clear A-to-B move (versus an A v1.0-to-A v2.0), they are far more likely to see this as different instead of a flavor of the week, or worse, more of the same.

Don't water down the message. Part of the power of this research (as confirmed by early adopters of the model itself) is the *contrast* it offers between the old way and the new, more effective way to sell. Aligning the message to the old way of selling means that reps *may* adjust behavior at the margins, but most will fail to see it for what it is and won't do anything differently as a result. The best gauge of the power of your message to the organization is how many people *disagree* with you and want to debate—this is probably true of anything, but it's especially true when you're talking about driving change in the sales organization, whose inertia around legacy ways of doing things can be hard to break, to put it mildly.

If you are a sales leader or a training professional, in other words, you need to be a Challenger yourself. Teach reps to value the change you are selling to them. Picking agreeable terms that don't ruffle feathers might make everybody in the organization feel good, but rest assured, few will remember what you said and you will be far less likely to compel change as a result. And, as we know, the same is true for reps presenting to customers—it is the Challengers' desire to create constructive tension (often with specific language and data that reframe the customer's view of things) that creates a differentiated sales experience, one that ultimately builds more loyal customers.

Beware the "Challenging Won't Work Here" Trap

A question we get from our members who operate global sales organizations is whether the Challenger Selling Model is appropriate for non-Western markets. The root of this question is typically based on the concern that in certain markets, namely in Asia-Pacific, "challenging" is sometimes seen as aggressive, arrogant, and potentially offensive to customers.

We argue that one of the fundamental precepts of the Challenger model—that customers reward those organizations and those sales reps who bring *insight* to the table—is true regardless of where you sell or to whom you sell. This is corroborated not only by our own customer loyalty study, which included customers from around the world, but also by our members, many of whom have years of experience managing sales organizations in overseas markets. The desire for new ideas to help save money or make money is not limited to Western customers.

However, some concepts likely need to be finessed so sales reps and managers in certain geographic markets like Asia-Pacific don't reject them out of hand. We have found that some Asian sales organizations balk at the term "Challenger" and don't like the notion of "teaching" customers. Both the problem and the solution are semantic in nature. While we would argue for not watering down the Challenger message by giving it a different name, it is relatively easy to shift terms like "teaching" to "sharing and delivering insights."

One of our members shared her experiences presenting the Challenger work to her sales teams in China. She was surprised at the unenthusiastic response to her first few presentations. After three such sessions with local sales teams, she pulled one of her longtime direct reports aside to ask why the sales managers and reps didn't seem excited about the Challenger concept—after all, their peers in the United States and in Europe were really fired up about it. Her direct report explained that the sales teams *did* find the research interesting, but they were concerned about some of the language. He suggested a slight modification: Add the word "respectfully" before she said things like "teach," "challenge," or "take control." In the next session, with this slight modification, she found the sales teams *much* more engaged throughout the discussion—asking questions and talking openly about how to "respectfully challenge" their customers' thinking by bringing new insights to the discussion.

While challenging holds in non-Western markets, the *way* in which one challenges is probably a little different. The way that ideas are introduced to and discussed with the customer could vary based on cultural patterns of behavior, but this is no different from the way selling has always been done. While the basic principles are the same for every culture, the execution varies to meet local norms of behavior and dialogue. In other words, challenge but tailor accordingly!

Start Now

We said it before, but we'll say it again. If you are looking for a quick fix, look elsewhere. We have seen quick wins from rolling out the Challenger Selling Model—one company we helped implement the model reported 6 percent market share growth in twelve months, and another brought in their largest-ever deal within a quarter of rolling out Challenger training—but getting it fully "installed" won't happen overnight.

The Challenger Selling Model is a commercial transformation. Getting it right requires significant changes to the way sales and marketing interact, to the kind of tools you arm your reps with, the sort of reps you recruit, the kind of training you deliver to them, and the way managers interact with them. Getting this right—all of it—is hard. The majority of the companies profiled in this book would tell you that this transformation took not months, but years, and that their work continues to this day. As we said earlier in this book, the Challenger Selling Model is a new operating system for the commercial organization, not just another "bolt-on" application to the existing system.

It's not all bad news, however. Moving now means changing the way your reps interact with customers before your competitors do—and the data is very clear about what customers want. While the competition sends out Relationship Builders equipped to have only fact-, feature- and benefit-focused conversations, your Challenger reps are leading with insights, teaching customers about problems they didn't even know they had. The competition's reps will earn glances at the clock and disingenuous offers to "get back to them on their proposals." Your reps will earn more time from the customer, open invitations to come back, and sincere promises to take action. While the competition focuses its energies on *finding* customers, you will be out there *making* customers.

CHALLENGING BEYOND SALES

THE OBSERVATION CAME up at a lunch break at one of our member meetings in late 2009. We'd just finished presenting the Challenger findings to the thirty members or so in attendance, and the head of sales from a high-tech company leaned over and said, "You know, I find this Challenger stuff really fascinating—not because of what it says about salespeople, which is interesting, but more because it's the story of my career at this company."

Puzzled, we asked what he meant. "I haven't always been in sales," he explained. "I grew up in engineering but then spent time in the IT department, HR, and marketing. Sales is actually a new thing for me. What's interesting is that I would think the Challenger approach would apply to almost any of these functions." He continued, "When I was in IT, we were always talking about how to improve the ability of our folks to deliver *value* to our internal business customers . . . you know, to get out of 'order taker' mode and be seen as a trusted adviser, a consultant to the line, that sort of thing. Then, when I went to HR, it was the same discussion. Ditto for marketing. That's really what Challenger is all about . . . and that's not a problem only for sales reps. Have you guys thought of looking at this model in a non-sales setting?"

In fact, we hadn't, but our colleagues here at CEB have.

One of the great things about being part of a company like ours is that we have hundreds of colleagues around the world producing cutting-edge content for every corporate function imaginable. CEB Sales Leadership Council is one offering of our broader Sales & Service practice, one of eight corporate function practice areas across the company. Our other practices are in human resources; finance; innovation and strategy; legal, risk, and compliance; information technology; marketing and communications; and procurement and operations. All told, our company serves more than 240,000 business leaders across roughly 10,000 organizations in over 110 countries. That's a pretty wide angle to get on any business issue. So we picked up the phone and asked a number of our senior research colleagues and even some of our members, "Does the Challenger model apply in your world?"

What we learned was fascinating and suggests that this member might be on to something.

INTERNAL BUSINESS CUSTOMERS WANT INSIGHT TOO

By this point in the book, one thing that should be very clear is that what customers want more than anything else is for their suppliers to deliver insight to them—new ideas for saving money and making money that they'd not previously considered. It should come as no surprise that *internal* business customers want—or perhaps more appropriately, expect—the same thing of the corporate functions they work with.

Take, for example, HR. Through our HR practice, we have found that of all of the things that *could* account for recruiter effectiveness, it was the recruiter's ability to be a strategic adviser that accounted for 52 percent of effectiveness, compared with 33 percent that was driven by pipeline management and only 15 percent by the ability to manage the recruiting process. That's a striking finding. But what was more interesting was that only 19 percent of recruiters would currently qualify as true talent advisers to the business partners, according to heads of recruiting.

We've heard something very similar from our colleagues in CEB's IT practice. Last year, they looked at the question of how to improve the value that IT business liaisons (the IT staff who interface with line executives) deliver to their internal customers. Historically, this has been an area where IT departments have a lot of opportunity to improve.

They found that between 2007 and 2009, the percentage of business leaders rating their IT departments as "effective" at applying IT capabilities to business needs actually *declined*. In 2007, 31 percent of business leaders rated IT as "effective," but that number shrank to 26 percent in 2009. And it's not just senior leaders who think IT has room to improve; it's end users too. In a 2009 survey of more than 5,000 end users, we found that a stunning 76 percent *disagreed* with the statement that their job performance had improved because of a new system delivered by IT.

What we've found in IT is very similar to what we've found in recruiting and, of course, sales. Business customers want their IT business liaisons to bring them new ideas for how they can use technology to save money or make money. Efficient service delivery is all well and good, but what the business really values is insight into how they can compete more effectively.

Think about the parallels here. In our study of business customers, we found that 53 percent of loyalty was driven by the sales experience—namely the supplier's ability to deliver unique insight to the customer. These are very similar results to what we learned makes recruiters and IT business liaisons effective in their jobs. We also found that the reps who can deliver the unique insights customers are looking for—the Challenger reps—represent only 27 percent of all salespeople. Again, this is very similar to what our colleagues in recruiting and IT found.

BREAKING OUT OF ORDER-TAKER MODE

The corollary to being a Relationship Builder as a salesperson is to be seen as an "order taker" in other functional areas. We heard this time and again in our discussions with our CEB colleagues.

Colleagues from our Marketing & Communications practice, told us that communicators have long been fighting to move upstream in the value chain with their business customers. They want to move from "managing the message" to "managing the debate," but in order to do this, they need to practice something called "tactical deafness." In other words, heads of communications try to get their teams to purposefully *ignore* the specific tactic a business customer is asking for (e.g., "We need a press release on X") so that they can instead dig for the strategic reason *driving* the request ("We need to make sure our competitors see that we've moved into this space"). Doing this, a savvy communicator will often identify opportunities to deliver much greater value than what could have been accomplished just by "taking the order."

One of the best practices we teach members in our communications program comes from the VP of communications at an auto manufacturer. She taught her team to practice a five-step process designed to enforce rigorous critical thinking about partners' business problems. The process ensures that corporate communications' solutions target the most significant drivers of partners' performance gaps. Communications' use of the problem-solving process has strengthened the quality and impact of its solutions to partners' business problems and has increased the transparency of communications' contribution to performance improvements. In this way, this practice has helped position the function as a consultative partner capable of driving business results.

Sometimes the stakes are even higher. Companies rely on central functions like strategy, R&D, and procurement not just to take orders, but to make sure the business is thinking through its assumptions rigorously—whether those assumptions pertain to a new market opportunity or the price to be paid for critical inputs and materials.

Colleagues from our Procurement & Operations practice recently looked at how Purchasing leaders can equip their managers to effectively challenge line customers' deeply held beliefs. "In order to generate truly innovative ideas," our colleagues explained to us, "procurement must be able to understand the strategy and—more important—understand the assumptions that underlie it. With this knowledge, procurement can go beyond analyzing spend data to find other areas that could benefit from procurement's expertise. After learning the assumptions that underlie the business's strategy, procurement *should* push back on weak points to determine which parts of the strategy are based on false or questionable premises. *Challenging* these ideas and coming back to the business with a superior alternative will generate significant improvements to the company."

R&D is also an area where questioning assumptions and deeply held beliefs is of paramount importance, lest the organization end up blind-sided by unseen risks or be held captive by its own biases. To help them emerge successfully from the current wobbly economy, companies are looking for "transformational innovation" from their R&D groups—in other words, they're looking to feed the front end of the innovation pipeline. The payoff for getting this right is huge for a company: Collegues from our Innovation & Strategy practice found that R&D organizations that excel at seeding the growth portfolio with transfor-mational ideas generate *double* the new product sales relative to peers. In addition, transformational ideas have development cycles that are 11 percent faster than their competitors', since ideas that are well scoped and connected to market needs require less rework.

Our colleagues found that of all of the competencies for an R&D department to possess, "strategic influence"—that is, the ability of R&D to influence corporate and business strategies—delivered the greatest return in terms of enabling these transformational ideas. At the same time, nearly 70 percent of R&D heads our company surveyed reported that their teams lacked this important capability.

The issue here, for most organizations, is that the front end of the innovation funnel is where many good ideas go to die. Companies, it turns out, frequently miss out on transformational innovations due to R&D's inability to convince business partners of an idea's merit. The reason so few ideas are successful in the market is often because R&D scopes out good ideas, fails to convince the business of the relevance of ideas, or is unable to connect ideas to market needs.

In response, CEB has pulled together a series of best practices—not unlike what we've delivered in support of the Challenger Selling Model. The practices they've been out teaching their members have to do with new ways of arming the R&D team to challenge the entrenched assumptions of the business, avoid knee-jerk rejection of new opportunities, and compress the time it takes to collect feedback on early-stage ideas.

SPEAKING THE LANGUAGE OF THE BUSINESS

A common, though very tactical, pitfall we see internal business functions struggle with is their inability to communicate to business partners in terms they understand. More often than not, this is because folks at the corporate center are experts in their specific domain area, and while their knowledge of their functions—be it legal, IT, or HR—instills confidence in business partners, it does little to assist these functional experts in communicating compelling ideas and insights.

One financial services company we work with in our Sales & Service practice described for us what is an evergreen problem for customer service: getting the business to take action on customer complaints. Historically, they had presented complaint data in "call center terms," that is to say, in terms of number of calls, total time required to handle complaints, etc. But they found it difficult to break through with business customers. In response, they developed a "complaint-to-market impact" model that helped them calculate, for any customer complaint, what the likely financial impact would be for the company. Suddenly, business customers were all ears. According to the VP of customer service, "There are always customer issues that end up ingrained in the organization. This data—because it's in clear terms you can't ignore—really puts the issues right in your face. It helps us find systematic issues and convince others that it's worth partnering with us to fix them."

One of the worst offenders when it comes to technical jargon is legal, as technical a function as exists within the large corporate enterprise. A member who works with our colleagues in the Legal, Risk & Compliance practice told us that it's an area where he spends a fair bit of time and energy developing his team: "Skills attorneys learn in law school aren't the ones that will make them effective in a business setting. As law students, attorneys learn to write long, technical briefs. These are great for a judge, but they're terrible for a businessperson. We spend a lot of time on how you communicate to your business partners. I even bring in a communications coach to help them stop saying things like 'whereas' and 'heretofore' in their presentations. They've got to be able to engage with the business if they're going to be successful in an in-house legal setting."

This particular general counsel goes on to explain that it's not just technical jargon that gets in the way of attorneys' being effective in dealing with business customers; it's also their natural predisposition to want to "call balls and strikes" rather than give the business options that will help them make decisions: "Attorneys like to give gray answers—this decision 'might go for you or against you'—but that's not helpful to our customers. They can't make informed decisions with guidance like that." To help get his attorneys out of this mindset, he actually enlists the help of an outside expert who teaches litigation risk projections. "We don't have a crystal ball," he explains, "but we can give probabilities on decisions and estimates for potential damages. That's a lot more helpful to our business partners than saying a judgment 'could go either way.'"

EARNING A SEAT AT THE TABLE

Just getting rid of jargon and speaking in business terms might make the business listen to what you have to say, but it's unlikely to earn you an invitation to critical strategy meetings or make you a "must-have" voice at high-risk decision points. It's a way to not get ignored, but probably not a way to get sought out. To earn a "seat at the table," corporate center staff need to deliver compelling insights, and there aren't a lot of second and third chances given out here by busy line executives.

One of our favorite tactics for picking those occasions to "plant the flag" and make your team an indispensable business partner comes from our colleagues in the Marketing & Communications practice. Market researchers struggle with all of the problems we've discussed so far—they have, in most companies, propagated their own reputations as nothing more than "order takers," and they struggle to relate to business partners because of how steeped they tend to be in their own technical domains.

The practice in question comes from a high-tech company whose research leader had identified a number of opportunities for market research to substantially inform strategic debates going on at the highest levels of the company. The problem was that the market research function was newly centralized in the company and hadn't yet earned a seat at the table with these other senior leaders. As the head of research at the time explained, "We were able to identify areas where we could advise the firm strategically but were not yet in a position to be heard by management. They first needed to experience exactly what a strategic adviser is capable of doing, so the challenge was finding the opportunity to show my group's abilities."

To make sure that his group put its best foot forward, he established a handful of criteria that would ensure they wouldn't waste an opportunity to make the right first impression with senior leadership: (1) The project had to correspond to an issue of significance on management's agenda; (2) there had to be a high likelihood that the research team would uncover significant insights; (3) the project had to be within the group's expertise; (4) there had to be a high probability of resolution to the issue; and (5) the project had to have low resource requirements. Sound familiar? The criteria of the head of market research bear a real resemblance to what makes for a good teaching pitch. In fact, some of them are identical to the SAFE-BOLD Framework we discussed in chapter 5.

The criteria helped the research department deliver compelling insights in their first presentation to the management team, ultimately doubling the number of strategic projects they were asked to complete and increasing the department's budget by 65 percent. "The trick," the director of the team explained, "is finding the right issue. Once you achieve those early successes, doors start opening and executives make time for the group because they know we are going to have something important to say."

A PERMANENT RESET?

At CEB, we offer a number of similar training programs for corporate center staff across our memberships. CEB HR and CEB Finance

Leadership Academies, for instance, are heavily focused on building consultative skills for high performers within these different corporate functions at our member companies. Similarly, our market research program offers consultative skills and presentation skills training. All of these offerings are consistently sold out, suggesting that this is—at least for now—a pressing issue for functional leaders. But will demand for these kinds of skills and capabilities fade?

It's hard to predict what skills will be in vogue in five or ten years in large companies, but we would argue that it's unlikely that business customers will lower the bar anytime soon for their corporate center colleagues. Internal customers, like outside ones, will continue to be open to new ideas for saving money or making money and they will reward suppliers—whether external suppliers or the corporate functions that support them internally—who bring insight to the table. While the business may have no option *but* to work with an internal supplier, they often hold the purse strings, and the gap between funding to keep the lights on and funding for large-scale projects and solutions can be quite wide indeed.

We suspect that the Challenger concept resonates so well with other functional areas beyond sales because it suggests a promising alternative to the current state in which many functional leaders find themselves today. Just like the supplier fighting for a customer's loyalty, functional leaders want—for themselves and their teams—a seat at the table where the biggest business decisions are made. The Challenger model offers at least a starting point for these teams to stand up and be counted in a way that is fundamentally different from the reactive, order-taking world.

ACKNOWLEDGMENTS

PRINCIPAL CONTRIBUTORS

While this book has two authors on the cover, it is, like all CEB studies, the product of an enormous team undertaking. At the top of the list of contributors are three individuals who, along with the authors, formed the core of the research team behind this work:

Karen Freeman

Karen served as research director for CEB Sales Leadership Council from 2008 to 2010 and was the driving force and principal thought leader behind the original Challenger study, *Replicating the New High Performer,* in 2009 as well as the follow-on manager effectiveness study, *Building Sales Managers for a Return to Growth* in 2010. It was her unfailing commitment to delivering the most powerful and provocative research possible—in effect, her ambition to push the thinking of even our most progressive members—that ultimately made the Challenger study the most successful ever delivered by CEB Sales Leadership Council. Karen has also served as research director for CEB Marketing Leadership Council, and was a recipient of the "Force of Ideas" award, one of the highest honors bestowed on a CEB employee, in 2010. She is currently CEB's managing director of learning and development.

Timur Hicyilmaz

Timur has served as CEB Sales Leadership Council head of quantitative research since 2005. In this capacity, he has been the quant "visionary," survey designer, and principal modeler and data analyst behind all of CEB Sales' major research initiatives, including all of the major quantitative studies that underpin the findings discussed in this book. Timur's keen quantitative skills are second only to his incredible capacity for using data to reframe the way managers think about their organizations and his amazing depth of knowledge in B2B sales and marketing. Timur currently serves as a senior director within the Marketing & Communications practice and Sales & Service practice of CEB, where he continues to oversee all of the practices' quantitative research. To this day, he is one of our most sought-after researchers for engaging in member conversations, especially around large-scale strategic issues.

Todd Burner

Todd Burner served as the day-to-day project manager on both the 2009 *Replicating* study as well as the 2010 *Building* study. As team leader, Todd devoted more time to these research studies—including countless early morning, late evening, and weekend hours—than anybody on the team. A perfectionist at heart, Todd held his team to an incredibly high bar, knowing that only the most insightful content was worthy of our members' time and attention. Without Todd's intellectual rigor, commitment to excellence, and dedication to his team, it is doubtful that these studies would have been delivered on time, let alone at the standard they were. A gifted business leader, Todd currently serves as a research director in CEB's IT practice.

WITH SINCERE THANKS

Beyond the principal contributors to this research, there is a long list of individuals and organizations without whose commitment and support this research and this book would never have seen the light of day.

First, we owe a tremendous debt of gratitude to the leadership of our firm, especially our chairman and CEO, Tom Monahan, and the general manager of our Sales & Service practice and Marketing & Communications practice, Haniel Lynn. It was their commitment to our company's core values, especially what we call the "Force of Ideas," that kept the organization steadfastly focused on delivering major, groundbreaking research to our members, even in the depths of the recession when it might have been easier and more expedient to focus resources elsewhere.

With the support of Tom, Haniel, and our company's senior leadership, we were able to concentrate the firepower of a truly awesome research team on discovering and defining the Challenger Selling Model. Specifically, we wish to thank current researchers Jamie Kleinerman, Victoria Koval, Patrick Loftus, Patrick Spenner, and Josh Setzer; we also wish to thank current CEB Sales Leadership Council director Nick Toman, who has continued to lead the team in exploring the Challenger Selling Model and building resources to help our members implement it within their own organizations.

We also owe a tremendous amount to a number of former CEB researchers who each had a profound impact on the work in this book: Mary Detterick, Brianna Goode, Jason Grimm, Rob Hamshar, Hadley Heffernan, Andrew Kent, Aaron Lotton, Ashok Nachnani, Laurel Nguyen, Woody Paik, Tom Svrcek, Alex Tserelov, and Barry Winer.

Beyond the research team, we are supported by an all-star cast of executive advisers who bring the content to life for our members. The advisory function, which is headed by Tom Disantis for our Sales & Service practice and Katherine Evans for our Marketing & Communications practice, plays a critical role in the research process at CEB. In addition to Tom and Katherine, advisers who've heavily influenced this work include Dave Anderson, Anthony Anticole, Anthony Belloir, Jonathan Dietrich, Michael Hubble, Doug Hutton, Meta Karagianni, Rick Karlton, Matt Kiel, Ted McKenna, Peter Pickus, and Stacey Smith.

Where our member advisers leave off, our professional services team delivering CEB sales effectiveness solutions picks up. They customized engagement-level support to companies looking to implement any and all of the elements of the Challenger Selling Model. Led by Executive Director Nathan Blain, Practice Leader Simon Frewer, and Member Services Leader Sean Carr, the team is a world-class outfit, and the offering they have created in this space, the Challenger Development Program, is the envy of the industry.

Beyond these three individuals, many collegues from our professional services team including Joe Bisagna, Charlie Dorrier, and Jason Robinson—provided ongoing feedback on this work. On this point, Jessica Cash deserves a special thank-you for spending countless hours with this manuscript, helping us to significantly sharpen the teaching and insights contained herein. We also owe a tremendous amount to the facilitators who deliver CEB sales effective solutions—former sales and marketing leaders from our member companies, such as Tyrone Edwards, former head of North American sales at Merck, and Drew Pace, former head of sales at Bank of New York Mellon—who have continued to help us spread the word about the Challenger Selling Model and refine our thinking on what it means to take control of the customer conversation.

Ours is a unique craft and we and our teams rely heavily on the thought leadership and mentorship of those in our company who are best at what we do. Eric Braun is the head of research for our Sales & Service practice and Marketing & Communications practice and has been intimately involved in the Challenger research, alternately serving not just as chief of research quality control but as insight "Zen master" to our team. His fingerprints are all over this research, and the end result is much better for it.

Before Eric assumed this role, we had the privilege of studying under several research legends and masters of the "CEB Way," including Pope Ward, Tim Pollard, Derek van Bever, and Chris Miller. At different points in time over the past decade, these individuals taught us what it means to deliver research and insight worthy of our members' time and attention.

Last but not least, we are indebted to our own commercial team at CEB. Very early on, we were fortunate to be able to tap into the experiences and insights of our own "homegrown" Challengers such as Kevin Hart and Kristen Rachinsky. These individuals let us sit in on their sales calls and endured our many questions about why they sell the way they do.

Outside of CEB, we of course owe thanks to Neil Rackham, author of *SPIN Selling* and numerous other renowned works in the field, for his time and thoughtful consideration throughout this project. We are honored to be associated with Neil, the "professor emeritus" of the sales world.

All of our work at CEB is inspired by our members. They direct us to their most pressing issues, give generously of their time so that we can learn how these issues manifest for them and their commercial organizations, allow us to survey their reps, managers, and even customers, and, when called upon, to profile their best practices and tactics so that other members might avoid reinventing the wheel.

Within a membership that now spans hundreds of companies and thousands of individual sales and marketing leaders, we would like to specifically thank a few of our current and former members for their above-and-beyond contributions to this research:

Deb Oler, vice president and general manager of Grainger Brand, has been on the Challenger journey since long before it had a name. Her organization's many accomplishments and contributions to the Challenger Selling Model have been discussed in detail in this book, and Deb herself has been unfailingly generous with her time since we first stumbled upon her groundbreaking sales approach in late 2007. A true "guru" in her profession, she has continued to challenge us to further define the Challenger model and ask what's next for B2B sales and marketing.

Kevin Hendrick is senior vice president of sales for ADP's North American Employer Service business. A true first mover, Kevin has taken the Challenger Selling Model and applied it to his organization as quickly as we've been able to turn out the research. The tremendous success he's seen with the model aside, Kevin has been an invaluable resource to our team. Having a member who is so eager to apply the insights from our work and report back what he's learned has helped to ensure that this work stays grounded in the realities of B2B sales and marketing and that its lessons stay practical, as opposed to simply theoretical.

Finally, we wish to thank Dan James, former CSO of DuPont, who has been a guiding light for us from day one of this journey. As one of our leading members, Dan has given countless hours of his own time to help guide this research and provide feedback on it. While CSO, Dan gave us access to his reps, managers, and customers. He also agreed to be profiled for several best practices he and the DuPont team had architected. Since his retirement from DuPont, Dan has served as one of the principal facilitators of our CEB Challenger and Manager Development programs and has been an ongoing adviser on this book, conducting numerous interviews, helping us think through some of the trickier implementation issues in the Challenger model, and even editing the early manuscript of the book itself.

Speaking of editing, we would be remiss for not acknowledging the fantastic support of the many talented and dedicated professionals who helped shepherd this book through each phase of the journey: our agent, Jill Marsal of Marsal-Lyon; the terrific team at Portfolio, including our very talented editor, Courtney Young, and her editorial assistant, Eric Meyers; our very patient graphic designer, Tim Brown; our own excellent marketing and PR team at CEB, including Rory Channer, Ayesha Kumar-Flaherty, and Leslie Tullio; and last but not least, Gardiner Morse, senior editor at *Harvard Business Review*, for his support in helping us to unveil the Challenger Selling Model to the broader business community.

The final thank-you is the most important one. This research and this book would never have been possible were it not for the support and encouragement of our families. Anybody who has written a book knows that it's a big undertaking and that the price for the time it takes to get it done is often paid by those closest to the author.

Matt's beautiful and talented wife, Amy, and their four wonderful children, Aidan, Ethan, Norah, and Clara, showed nothing but patience and love for their father and helped keep him sane and grounded throughout this project. His only regret is that *The Challenger Sale* is unlikely to be included in the *Magic Tree House* series, and thus is likely to go unread by the Dixon children for the foreseeable future.

Brent can only wonder at his amazing wife, Ute, whose patience knows no bounds despite being sorely tested at times, and his two beautiful daughters, Allie and Kiera, who challenge him to see the world anew every single day. May you grow up to be Challengers in whatever you choose to do. But first . . . we're going to Disney World.

Excerpt from the Challenger Coaching Guide

TEACH

Pre-call Planning Questions

- What business problem will you be focusing on with this customer? How do you know that this is of critical importance to them? How have you seen similar companies approach this problem?
- How new/intriguing will this insight be to the customer? Why hasn't the customer figured it out already?

Post-call Debriefing Questions

- How intrigued or provoked was your customer with the insight(s) you shared? How could you tell?

Challenger Coaching Exercise

Understand the context: Select one customer/prospective account and answer the following questions:

- What are the company's strategic objectives for the next one to three years?
- Where are they strongest against their competition? Where are they lagging?

- How does the role of your contact/target impact the company's strategic objectives and strengths/weaknesses?

As the coach, partner with the sales professional to identify opportunities to connect the customer's business opportunities with your company's strengths to craft a more compelling teaching conversation.

TAILOR

Pre-call Planning Questions

- What are some of the latest trends in this customer's industry? How would those trends affect the customer's company?
- What is unique about this company's position in the marketplace? Where are they most vulnerable?

Post-call Debriefing Questions

- What did you learn about the customer's economic drivers?
- What goals, motivations, or information did you encounter that you hadn't expected? How did you respond?

TAKE CONTROL

Pre-call Planning Questions

- What are your next steps to ensure that the purchase process moves forward?
- What is your understanding of the customer's buying process?

Post-call Debriefing Questions

- What did this conversation do to move the sale forward?
- During moments of tension, was your gut feeling to defuse the tension or press on? What did you do?
- What are your next steps?

Download a more comprehensive guide at www.thechallengersale.com

Including:
- Coaching and development exercises
- Detailed Challenger behavior guides
- More pre- and post-call questions
- Tips to build a Challenger team
- Team meeting exercises
- Your role as a Challenger leader

Online materials guaranteed available until November 10, 2016.

Selling Style Self-Diagnostic

INSTRUCTIONS

Considering each of the statements below, score each one according to your agreement with how well it describes how you sell to your customers.

1 = Strongly disagree

2 = Disagree

3 = Neutral

4 = Agree

5 = Strongly agree

STATEMENT	SCORE
1) I often form enduring and useful relationships with customers.	
2) I can effectively offer my customers a unique perspective, teaching them new, unique insights that lead to my company's products and services.	
3) I am a true expert in the products and services I sell, comfortably exceeding the knowledge that any expert purchaser might have.	
4) I often risk disapproval in order to express beliefs about what is right for the customer.	
5) When negotiating with customers, I understand what drives value with different customers, adapting my message accordingly.	
6) I can identify the key drivers of a customer's business and use that information to customize my approach.	
7) When it comes to fulfilling customer requests, I usually resolve everything myself.	

STATEMENT	SCORE
8) In more difficult sales situations, I feel comfortable influencing the customer to make a decision.	
9) I can effectively discuss pricing and reimbursement concerns with my customers, on their own terms.	
10) I am likely to spend more time on preparation in advance of any sales calls or meetings than everybody else.	

SCORING GUIDE

- Add up your score for questions 2 and 3. Write that number in the "Teaches for Differentiation" box below.
- Add up your score for questions 5 and 6. Write that number in the "Tailors for Resonance" box below.
- Add up your score for questions 8 and 9. Write that number in the "Takes Control" box below.

If you rated yourself highly on questions 1, 4, 7, or 10, this means that you have natural sales tendencies in other sales profiles. (1 is Relationship Builder, 4 is Lone Wolf, 7 is Problem Solver, 10 is Hard Worker)

TEACHES FOR DIFFERENTIATION **TAILORS FOR RESONANCE** **TAKES CONTROL**

In each box:

- 8 or Above: Sounds like you're off to a great start; keep looking for ways to challenge your customers' thinking.
- 5 to 7: You have a good foundation to build on; target an area for development and start pushing yourself to challenge more.
- 4 or Below: This may be a slightly new approach for you; think about the area where you feel most comfortable and start your personal development there.

Challenger Hiring Guide:
Key Questions to Ask in the Interview

COMPETENCY	DEFINITION	SAMPLE INTER-VIEW QUESTIONS	EVALUATION GUIDELINES	RED FLAGS
Offers unique perspective	• Reframes and challenges the way customers view their businesses. • Aligns insights to key customer priorities and ties those insights back to the supplier's unique differentiators.	• How do you usually open a sales conversation with customers? • Describe a time you got a customer to think of their problem/need differently. • How do you decide what to include in your sales pitch? • How do you know that a customer is convinced by your line of thought? • Describe a time when your sales pitch fell flat. How did you react? • How do you adjust your sales pitch to different audiences?	• Structures the sales pitch to highlight customer benefits before supplier strengths. • Provides insights that are relevant to the customer's business and clearly tie back to the supplier's capabilities. • Adapts the sales pitch based on customer reactions.	• Sales pitch focuses on features and benefits. • Insights do not align with customer priorities. • Unable to articulate supplier differentiators. • Rep fails to make mid-pitch adjustments.

COMPETENCY	DEFINITION	SAMPLE INTER-VIEW QUESTIONS	EVALUATION GUIDELINES	RED FLAGS
Drives two-way communication	• Clearly articulates the supplier's value proposition and engages the customer in jointly addressing business priorities. • Reads nonverbal cues and identifies unanticipated customer needs. • Can coordinate and secure buy-in from internal stakeholders.	• How would you describe your typical relationship with a customer? • How do you get customers to talk about their business priorities? • What nonverbal cues do you look for during sales interactions? • Describe a time when you proactively addressed an unstated customer need. • How do you handle gatekeepers to gain access to busy executives? • Discuss a time when you overcame difficulty in coordinating across functions.	• Relationships are based on rep ability to teach to customer pain points. Modifies behavior based on nonverbal cues. • Has successfully coordinated across silos in response to complex customer needs.	• Does not seem open and/or approachable. • Inflexible, likes to have the last word. • Cannot pick up on body language. • Finds it hard to balance multiple relationships.
Knows customer value drivers	• Has a deep knowledge of customer business and can discuss issues from multiple angles. • Is comfortable talking to a wide range of decision influencers.	• What process do you follow to gain buy-in from customer stakeholders? • How do you identify key decision makers and influencers?	• Follows a structured process to identify key decision makers and their top priorities. • Tailors the sales pitch to unique customer requirements.	• Unaware of all parties involved in the deal. • Uses the same pitch for all customer contacts.

(continued)

COMPETENCY	DEFINITION	SAMPLE INTERVIEW QUESTIONS	EVALUATION GUIDELINES	RED FLAGS
	• Successfully links supplier capabilities to individual goals to overcome barriers to purchase.	• How do you decide what is and is not important to the decision maker(s)? • Describe your research process to learn about the customer's business. • How do you track potential enemy advocates in customer organizations? • Describe a time when your offerings did not match the customer's needs.	• Successfully transitions the relationship from supplier-vendor to a partnership in achieving customer objectives.	• Relationships remain transactional in nature. • Is unclear on customer's business priorities.
Can identify economic drivers	• Keenly tracks economic and industry activity and understands its implications for customer business, including potential new business opportunities. • Educates customers on industry trends and best practices adopted by peer companies.	• How has the current economic crisis affected an industry you sell into? • Describe a time you helped to shape or modify your customer's priorities. • Do your peers consider you an expert on economic/industry events? Why?	• Is knowledgeable about the economic and industry climate and relates that to the customer's business. • Customers proactively consult the rep during the planning process. • Frequently identifies new business opportunities that grow share of wallet.	• Does not possess in-depth industry knowledge. • Cannot relate economic events to customer goals. • Has failed to create new customer opportunities. • Cannot advise customers on business priorities.

COMPETENCY	DEFINITION	SAMPLE INTER-VIEW QUESTIONS	EVALUATION GUIDELINES	RED FLAGS
		• Which resources do you leverage to learn about the business environment? • Give an example of a new customer opportunity you identified and pursued. • Narrate a time you shared an industry best practice with a customer.		
Is comfortable discussing money	• Knows how supplier and competitor offerings are priced and is aware of the customer's budget. • Clearly links the value of the supplier's products and services with the deal price to overcome pricing objections. • Recognizes when to walk away from a deal.	• Talk about a time when you successfully pushed through a price increase. • What is your response to customers demanding pricing concessions? • Describe a time when you successfully negotiated on unclear price guidelines. • What is your reaction to a competitor who consistently undercuts your prices? • Describe a time when you walked away from a deal because of price.	• Comfortable talking about price at any stage of the sales cycle and does not depend on absolute pricing guidelines. • Gets customers to see beyond price and appreciate the supplier's unique differentiators. • Has closed deals with customers at a significant profit.	• Cannot clearly justify price with value. • Unaware of customer's purchasing ability. • Frequently concedes on pricing and discounts.

(continued)

COMPETENCY	DEFINITION	SAMPLE INTER-VIEW QUESTIONS	EVALUATION GUIDELINES	RED FLAGS
Can pressure the customer	• Understands the decision-making process and has the ability to influence key decision makers. • Preempts stakeholder objections and pushes the customer to a favorable outcome. • Develops customer advocates who sell and build consensus on the supplier's behalf.	• What is the one thing customers would associate with or say about you? • How do you build consensus among everyone involved in the sale? • Describe an instance where you managed to progress a stalled deal. • How have you dealt with customers annoyed by your negotiation tactics? • Describe a time you compromised to close a deal. What did you offer? • Discuss a time you convinced a customer advocate to sell on your behalf.	• Is a skilled negotiator who understands the decision-making process and the priorities of different stakeholders. • Generates consensus among stakeholders and independently closes deals. • Primarily targets advocates rather than seniormosts to secure buy-in.	• Overly aggressive or passive with customers. • Finds it hard to build stakeholder consensus. • Exercises price concessions to end negotiations. • Focuses exclusively on seniormost contacts.

STUART DIAMOND

GETTING MORE: How to Negotiate to Succeed in Work and Life

You're always negotiating. Whether making a business deal, talking to friends, booking a holiday or even driving a car, negotiation is going on: it's the basic form of all human interaction. And most of us are terrible at it.

Experts tell us to negotiate as if we live in a rational world. But people can be angry, fearful and irrational. To achieve your goals you have to be able to deal with the unpredictable.

In *Getting More*, negotiation expert Stuart Diamond reveals the real secrets behind getting more in any negotiation – whatever more means to you.

Stuart Diamond is the world's leading negotiator. He runs the most popular course at Wharton Business School, advises companies and governments on conflict resolution, and is the man who settled the Hollywood Writers' Strike.

'Practical, immediately applicable and highly effective' Evan Wittenberg, Head of Global Leadership Development, Google

'I rely on Stuart Diamond's negotiation tools every day' Christian Hernandez, Head of International Business Development, Facebook

'The world's best negotiator' *City AM*